SPYBOY™ YOUNG JUSTICE™

YOUNG SPIES LIKE US

Peter David
story

Pop Mhan and **Todd Nauck**
pencils

Norman Lee and **Jamie Mendoza**
inks

Guy Major
colors

Clem Robins
letters

Pop Mhan and
Todd Nauck
cover art

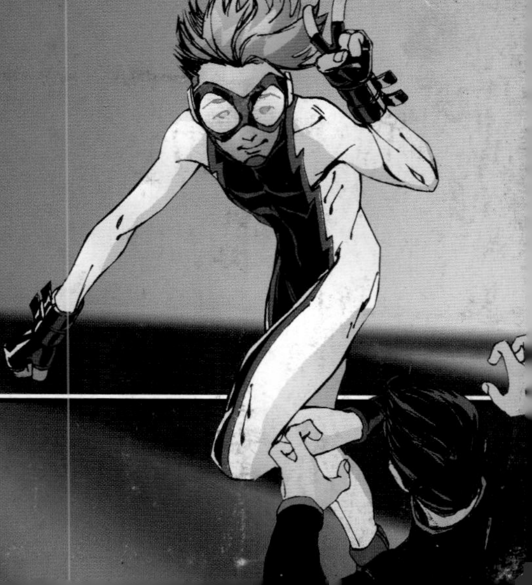

DARK HORSE COMICS®

David Nestelle
designer

Mark Cox
art director

Philip Wilson Simon
assistant editor

Phil Amara
editor

Mike Richardson
publisher

SpyBoy/Young Justice: Young Spies Like Us. Published by Dark Horse Comics, Inc., 10956 SE Main Street, Milwaukie, Oregon 97222. Copyright 2002 Dark Horse Comics, Inc. and DC Comics. SpyBoy™ and all related characters, their distinctive likenesses, and related indicia are trademarks of Dark Horse Comics, Inc. Young Justice™ and all related characters, their distinctive likenesses, and related indicia are trademarks of DC Comics. Dark Horse Comics® and the Dark Horse logo are trademarks of Dark Horse Comics, Inc., registered in various categories and countries. All rights reserved. No portion of this publication may be reproduced or transmitted, in any form or by any means, without the express written permission of the copyright holders. Names, characters, places, and incidents featured in this publication either are the product of the author's imagination or are used fictitiously. Any resemblance to actual persons (living or dead), events, institutions, or locales, without satirical intent, is coincidental.

This volume collects issues 1 – 3
of the Dark Horse comic-book series
SpyBoy/Young Justice.

published by
Dark Horse Comics, Inc.
10956 SE Main Street
Milwaukie, OR 97222

www.darkhorse.com

To find a comics shop in your area,
call the Comic Shop Locator Service
toll-free at 1-888-266-4226

First edition: December 2002
ISBN: 1-56971-850-4

10 9 8 7 6 5 4 3 2 1

PRINTED IN CHINA

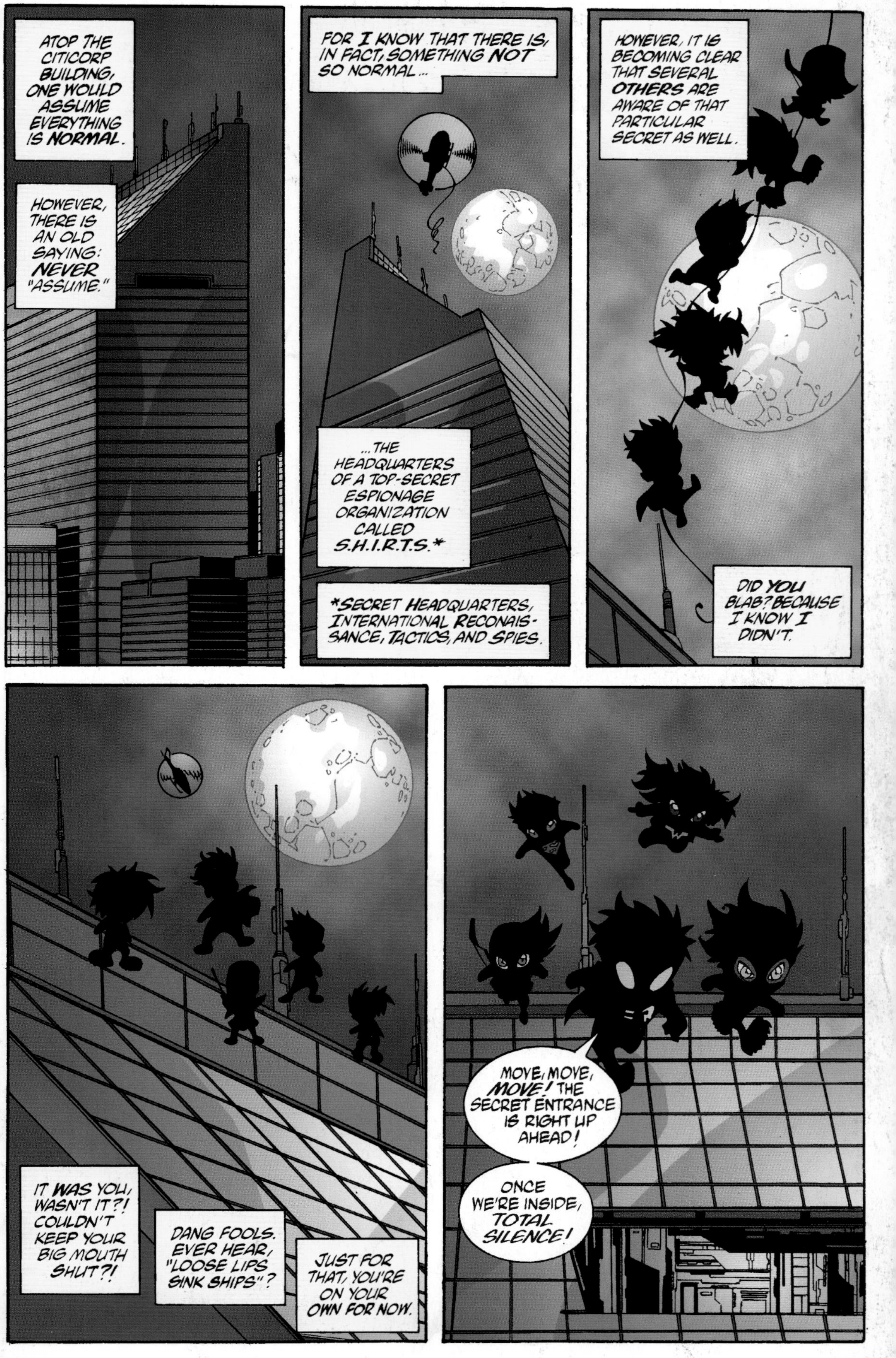
ATOP THE CITICORP BUILDING, ONE WOULD ASSUME EVERYTHING IS NORMAL.
HOWEVER, THERE IS AN OLD SAYING: NEVER "ASSUME."
FOR I KNOW THAT THERE IS, IN FACT, SOMETHING NOT SO NORMAL...
...THE HEADQUARTERS OF A TOP-SECRET ESPIONAGE ORGANIZATION CALLED S.H.I.R.T.S.*
*SECRET HEADQUARTERS, INTERNATIONAL RECONAISSANCE, TACTICS, AND SPIES.
HOWEVER, IT IS BECOMING CLEAR THAT SEVERAL OTHERS ARE AWARE OF THAT PARTICULAR SECRET AS WELL.
DID YOU BLAB? BECAUSE I KNOW I DIDN'T.
IT WAS YOU, WASN'T IT?! COULDN'T KEEP YOUR BIG MOUTH SHUT?!
DANG FOOLS. EVER HEAR, "LOOSE LIPS SINK SHIPS"?
JUST FOR THAT, YOU'RE ON YOUR OWN FOR NOW.
MOVE, MOVE, MOVE! THE SECRET ENTRANCE IS RIGHT UP AHEAD!
ONCE WE'RE INSIDE, TOTAL SILENCE!

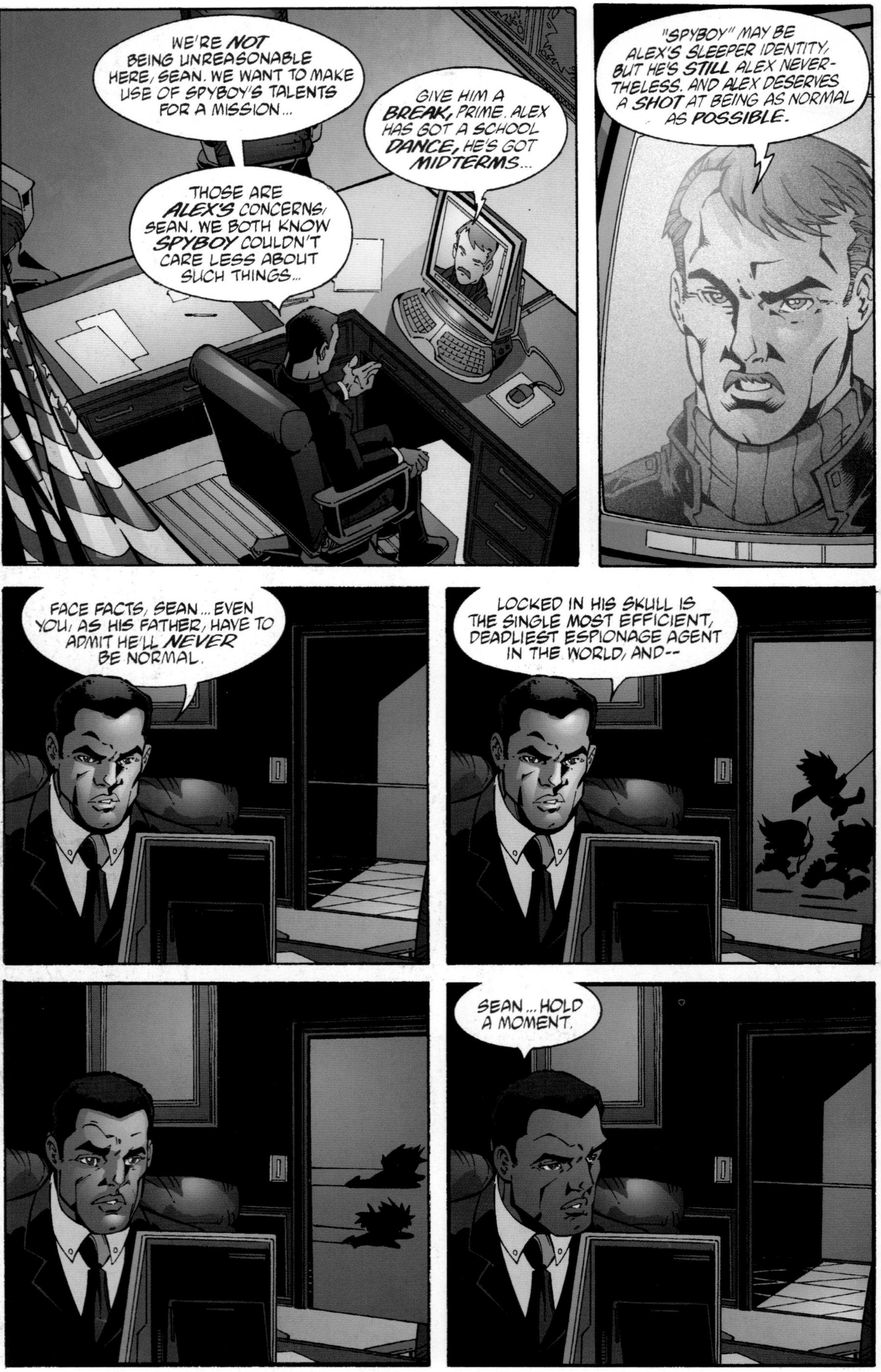
WE'RE NOT BEING UNREASONABLE HERE, SEAN. WE WANT TO MAKE USE OF SPYBOY'S TALENTS FOR A MISSION...
GIVE HIM A BREAK, PRIME. ALEX HAS GOT A SCHOOL DANCE, HE'S GOT MIDTERMS...
THOSE ARE ALEX'S CONCERNS, SEAN. WE BOTH KNOW SPYBOY COULDN'T CARE LESS ABOUT SUCH THINGS...
"SPYBOY" MAY BE ALEX'S SLEEPER IDENTITY, BUT HE'S STILL ALEX NEVERTHELESS. AND ALEX DESERVES A SHOT AT BEING AS NORMAL AS POSSIBLE.
FACE FACTS, SEAN... EVEN YOU, AS HIS FATHER, HAVE TO ADMIT HE'LL NEVER BE NORMAL.
LOCKED IN HIS SKULL IS THE SINGLE MOST EFFICIENT, DEADLIEST ESPIONAGE AGENT IN THE WORLD, AND--
SEAN... HOLD A MOMENT.

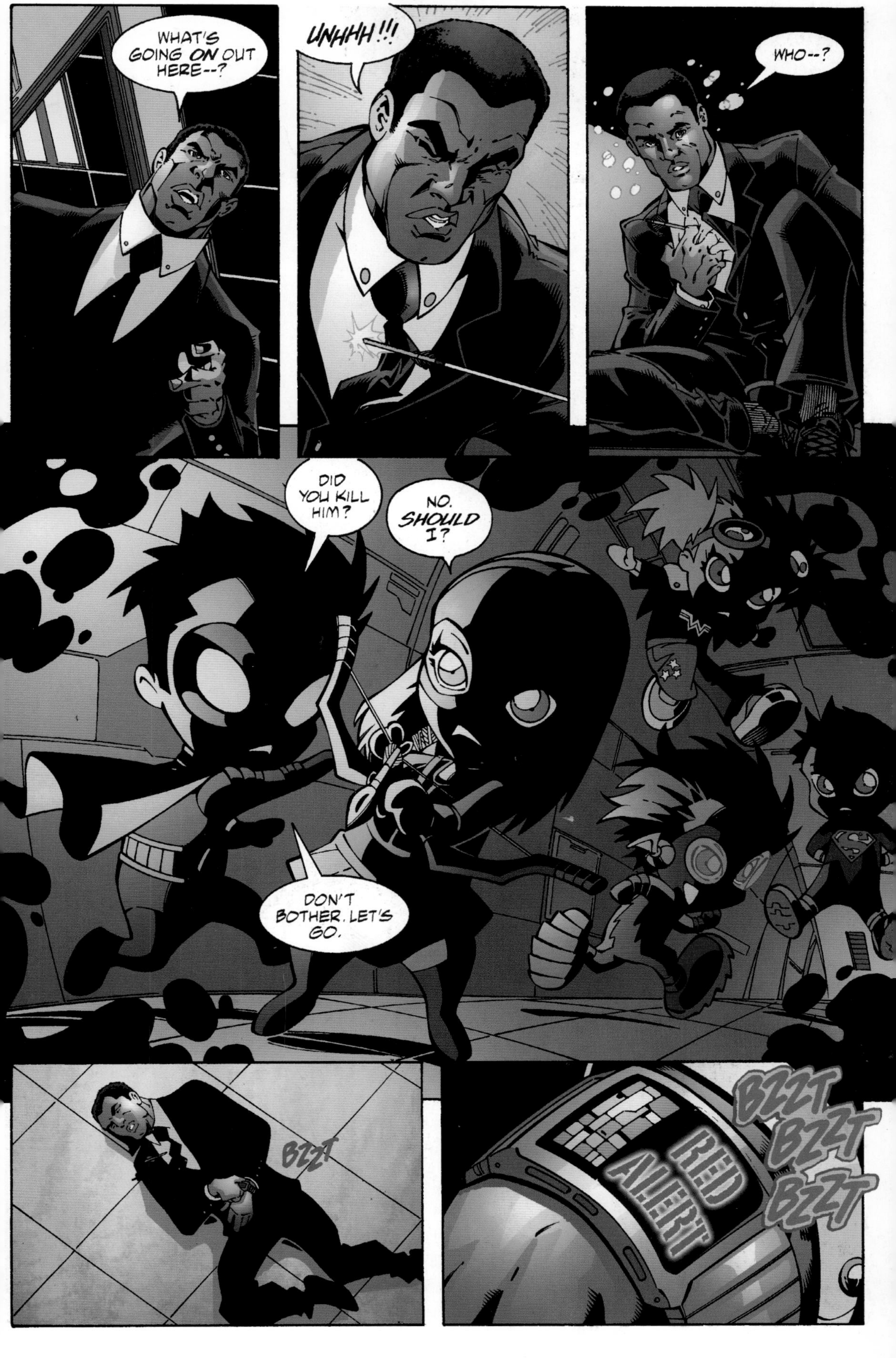
WHAT'S GOING ON OUT HERE--?
UNHHH!!!
WHO--?
DID YOU KILL HIM?
NO. SHOULD I?
DON'T BOTHER. LET'S GO.
BZZT
BZZT BZZT BZZT
RED ALERT

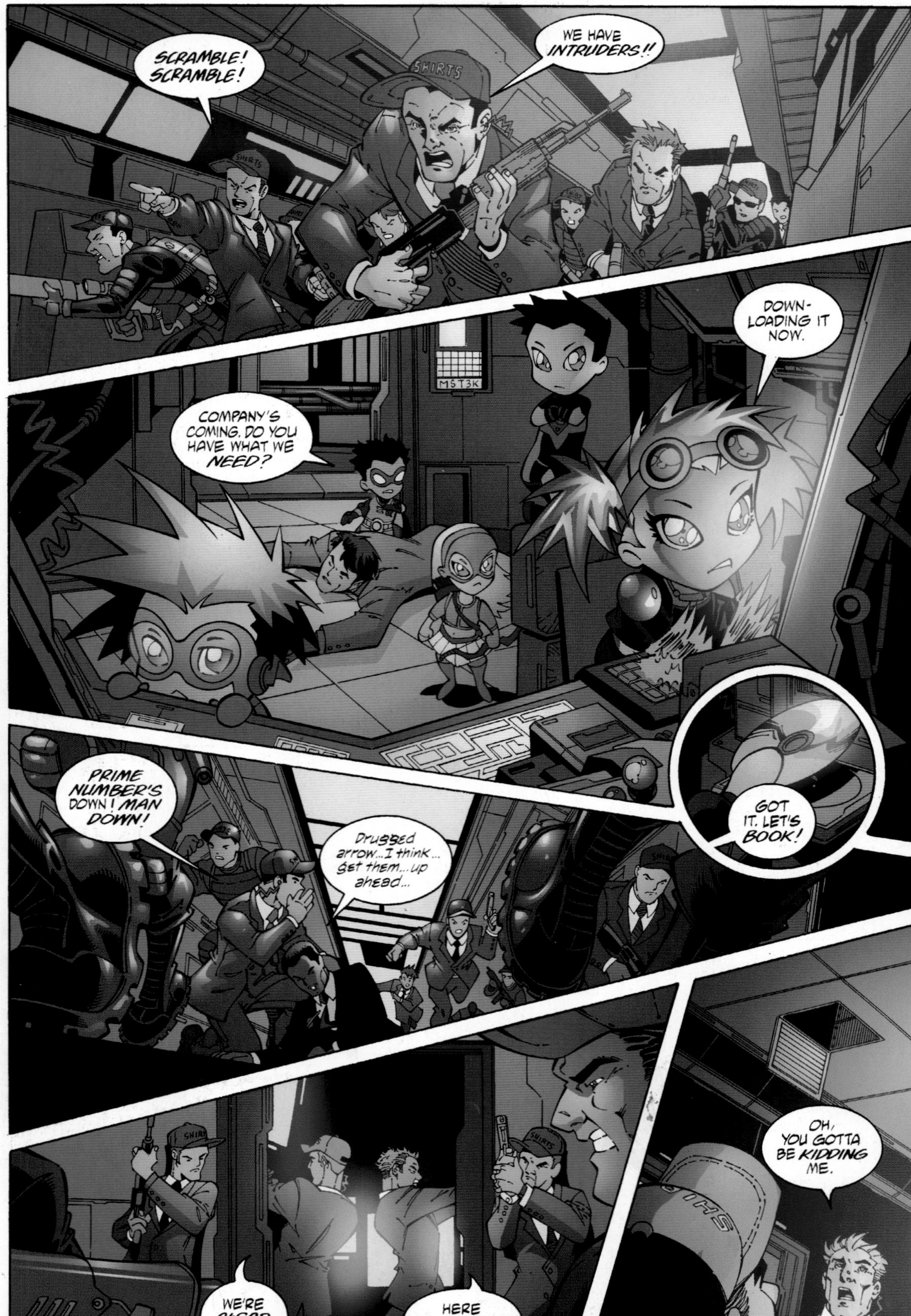
SCRAMBLE! SCRAMBLE!
WE HAVE INTRUDERS!!
SHIRTS
MST3K
COMPANY'S COMING. DO YOU HAVE WHAT WE NEED?
DOWN-LOADING IT NOW.
GOT IT. LET'S BOOK!
PRIME NUMBER'S DOWN! MAN DOWN!
Drugged arrow...I think... Get them...up ahead...
WE'RE CLEAR HERE!
HERE TOO! WHERE ARE--
OH, YOU GOTTA BE KIDDING ME.

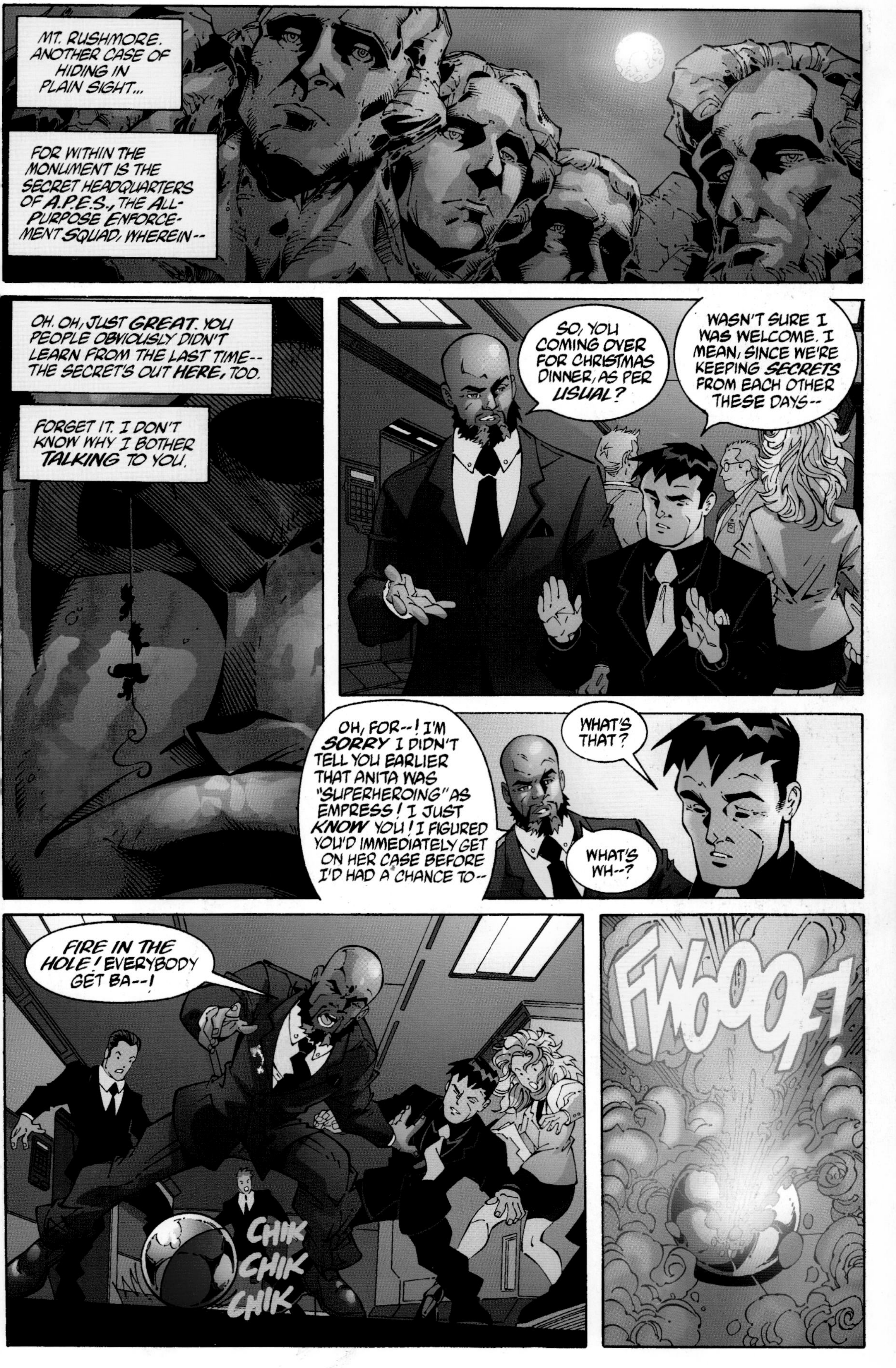

MT. RUSHMORE. ANOTHER CASE OF HIDING IN PLAIN SIGHT...
FOR WITHIN THE MONUMENT IS THE SECRET HEADQUARTERS OF A.P.E.S., THE ALL-PURPOSE ENFORCEMENT SQUAD, WHEREIN--
OH. OH, JUST GREAT. YOU PEOPLE OBVIOUSLY DIDN'T LEARN FROM THE LAST TIME-- THE SECRET'S OUT HERE, TOO.
FORGET IT. I DON'T KNOW WHY I BOTHER TALKING TO YOU.
SO, YOU COMING OVER FOR CHRISTMAS DINNER, AS PER USUAL?
WASN'T SURE I WAS WELCOME. I MEAN, SINCE WE'RE KEEPING SECRETS FROM EACH OTHER THESE DAYS--
OH, FOR--! I'M SORRY I DIDN'T TELL YOU EARLIER THAT ANITA WAS "SUPERHEROING" AS EMPRESS! I JUST KNOW YOU! I FIGURED YOU'D IMMEDIATELY GET ON HER CASE BEFORE I'D HAD A CHANCE TO--
WHAT'S THAT?
WHAT'S WH--?
FIRE IN THE HOLE! EVERYBODY GET BA--!
CHIK CHIK CHIK
FWOOOF!

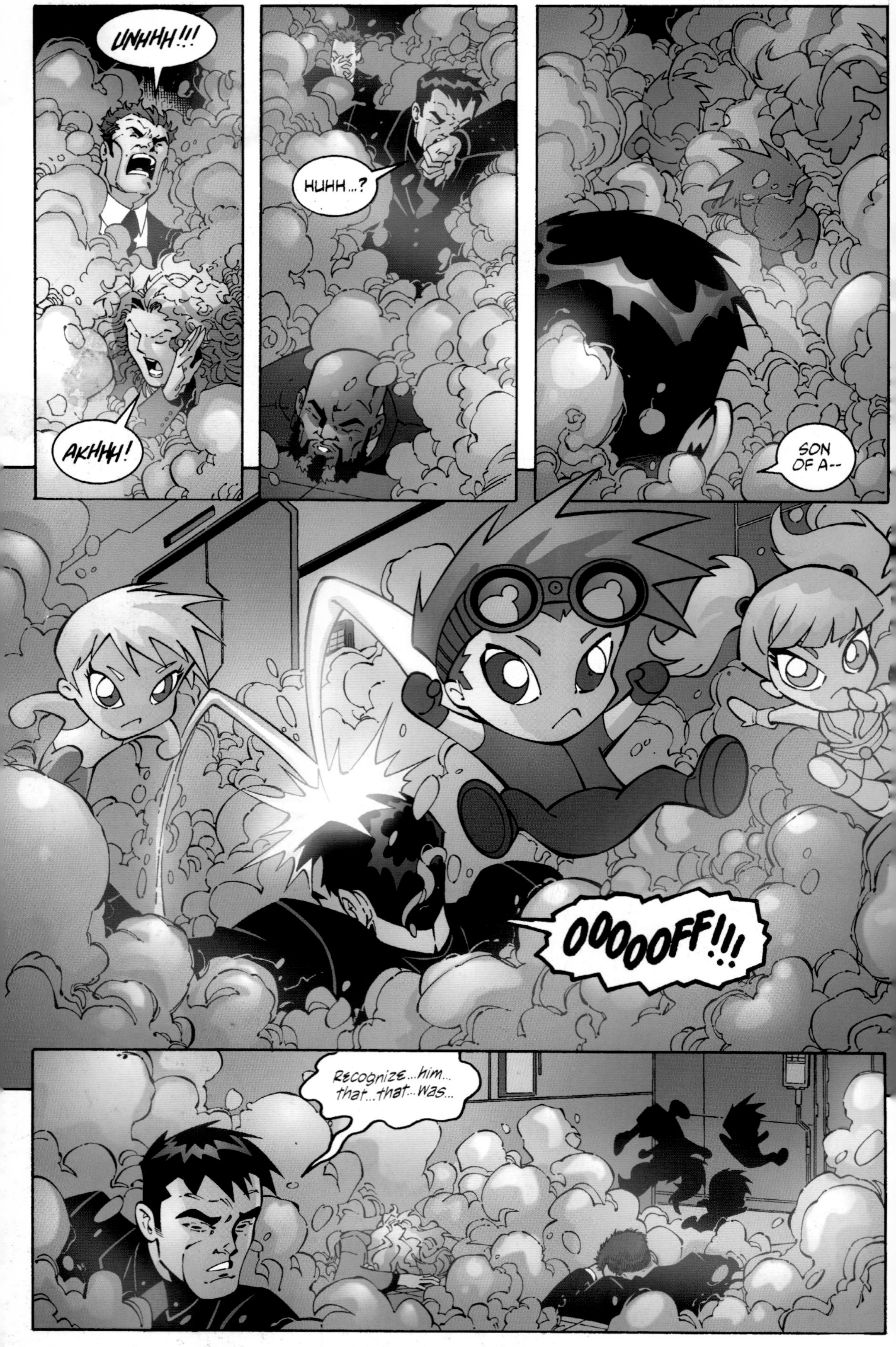
UNHHH!!!
AKHHH!
HUHH...?
SON OF A--
OOOOOFF!!!
Recognize...him... that...that...was...

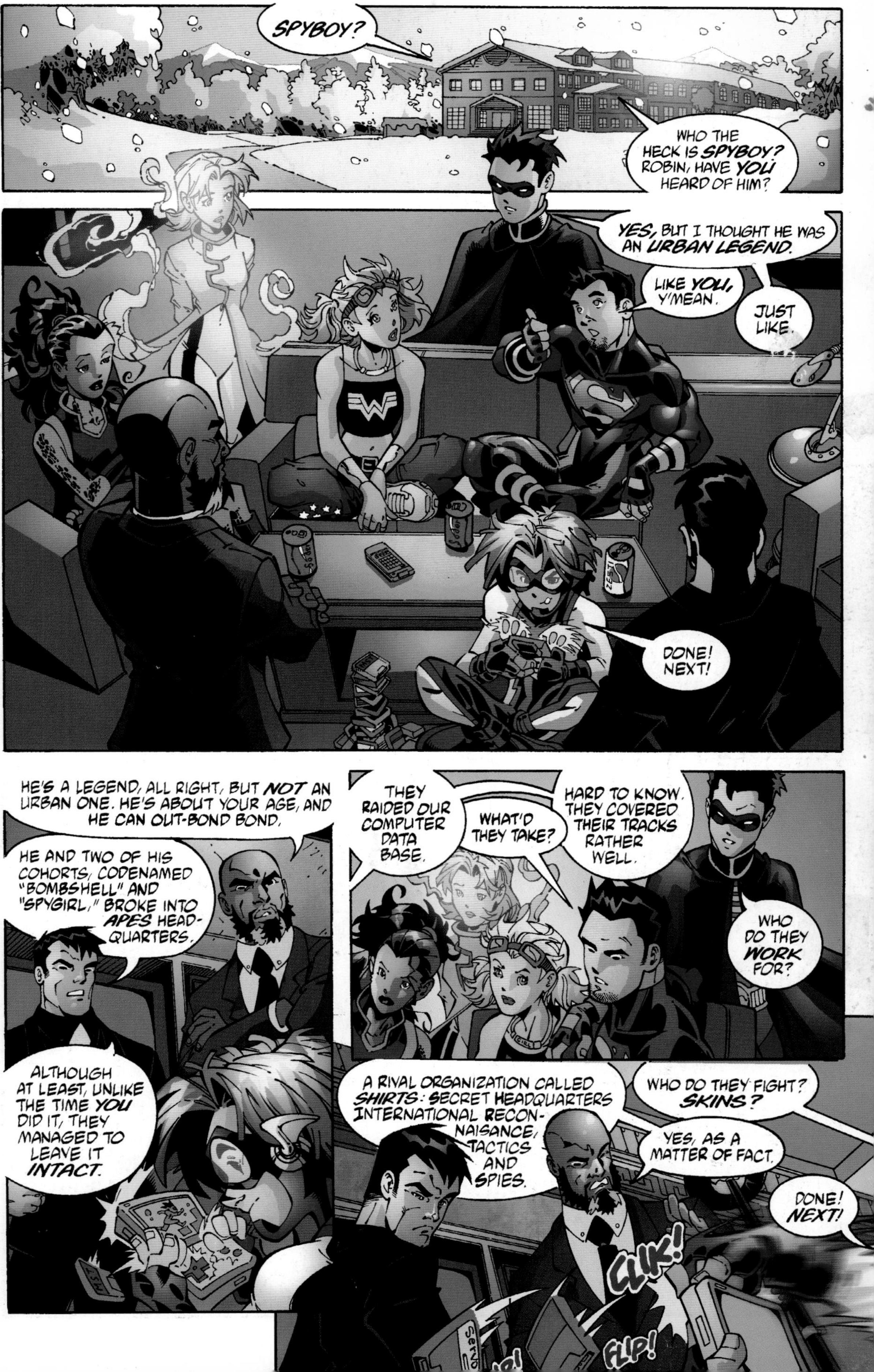

SPYBOY?
WHO THE HECK IS SPYBOY? ROBIN, HAVE YOU HEARD OF HIM?
YES, BUT I THOUGHT HE WAS AN URBAN LEGEND.
LIKE YOU, Y'MEAN.
JUST LIKE.
DONE! NEXT!
HE'S A LEGEND, ALL RIGHT, BUT NOT AN URBAN ONE. HE'S ABOUT YOUR AGE, AND HE CAN OUT-BOND BOND.
HE AND TWO OF HIS COHORTS, CODENAMED "BOMBSHELL" AND "SPYGIRL," BROKE INTO APES HEAD-QUARTERS.
ALTHOUGH AT LEAST, UNLIKE THE TIME YOU DID IT, THEY MANAGED TO LEAVE IT INTACT.
THEY RAIDED OUR COMPUTER DATA BASE.
WHAT'D THEY TAKE?
HARD TO KNOW. THEY COVERED THEIR TRACKS RATHER WELL.
WHO DO THEY WORK FOR?
A RIVAL ORGANIZATION CALLED SHIRTS: SECRET HEADQUARTERS INTERNATIONAL RECON-NAISANCE, TACTICS AND SPIES.
WHO DO THEY FIGHT? SKINS?
YES, AS A MATTER OF FACT.
DONE! NEXT!
CLIK!
FLIP!

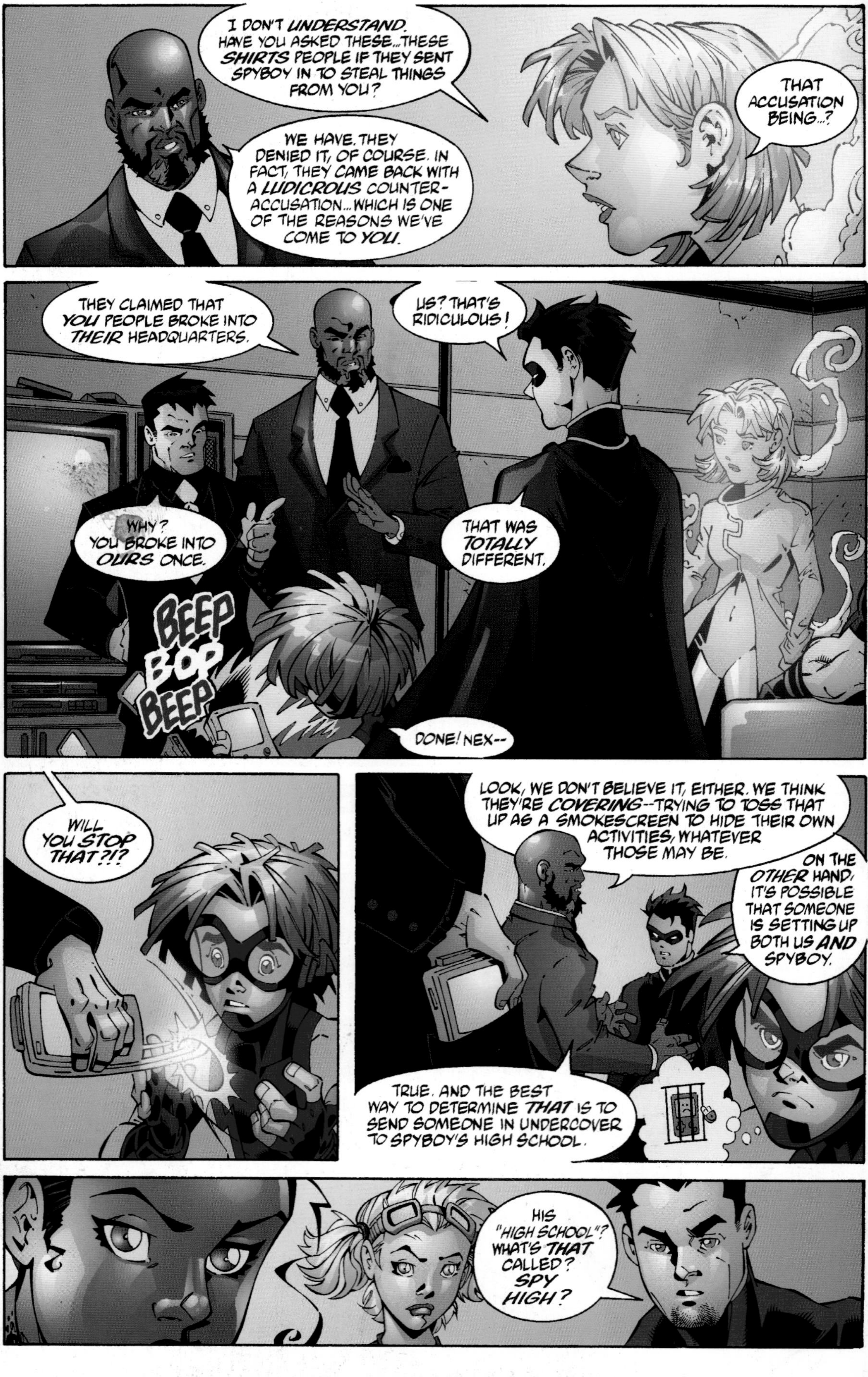
I DON'T UNDERSTAND. HAVE YOU ASKED THESE... THESE SHIRTS PEOPLE IF THEY SENT SPYBOY IN TO STEAL THINGS FROM YOU?
WE HAVE. THEY DENIED IT, OF COURSE. IN FACT, THEY CAME BACK WITH A LUDICROUS COUNTER-ACCUSATION... WHICH IS ONE OF THE REASONS WE'VE COME TO YOU.
THAT ACCUSATION BEING...?
THEY CLAIMED THAT YOU PEOPLE BROKE INTO THEIR HEADQUARTERS.
US? THAT'S RIDICULOUS!
WHY? YOU BROKE INTO OURS ONCE.
THAT WAS TOTALLY DIFFERENT.
BEEP BOP BEEP
DONE! NEX--
WILL YOU STOP THAT?!?
LOOK, WE DON'T BELIEVE IT, EITHER. WE THINK THEY'RE COVERING--TRYING TO TOSS THAT UP AS A SMOKESCREEN TO HIDE THEIR OWN ACTIVITIES, WHATEVER THOSE MAY BE.
ON THE OTHER HAND, IT'S POSSIBLE THAT SOMEONE IS SETTING UP BOTH US AND SPYBOY.
TRUE. AND THE BEST WAY TO DETERMINE THAT IS TO SEND SOMEONE IN UNDERCOVER TO SPYBOY'S HIGH SCHOOL.
HIS "HIGH SCHOOL"? WHAT'S THAT CALLED? SPY HIGH?

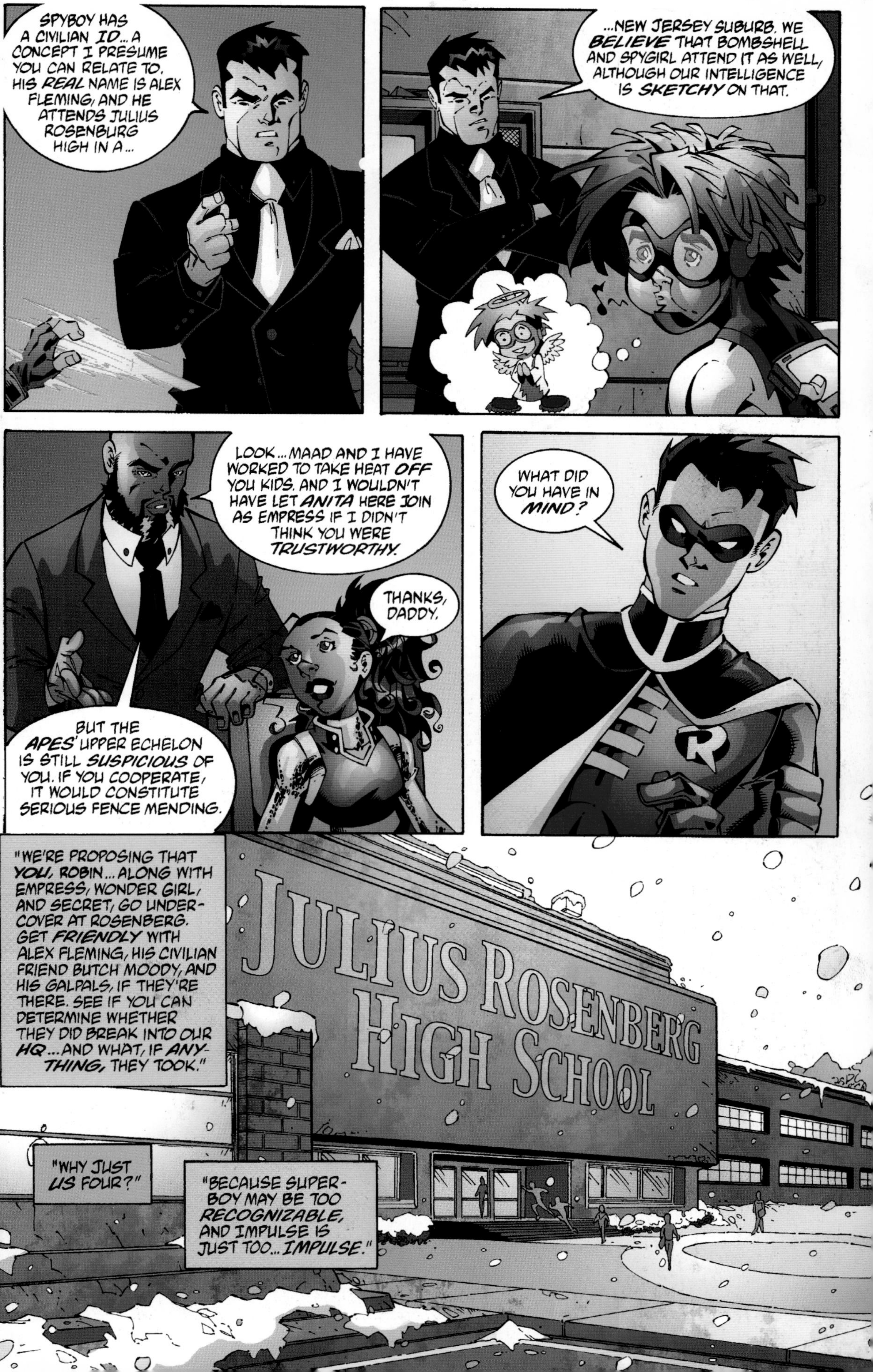
SPYBOY HAS A CIVILIAN ID... A CONCEPT I PRESUME YOU CAN RELATE TO. HIS REAL NAME IS ALEX FLEMING, AND HE ATTENDS JULIUS ROSENBURG HIGH IN A...
...NEW JERSEY SUBURB. WE BELIEVE THAT BOMBSHELL AND SPYGIRL ATTEND IT AS WELL, ALTHOUGH OUR INTELLIGENCE IS SKETCHY ON THAT.
LOOK... MAAD AND I HAVE WORKED TO TAKE HEAT OFF YOU KIDS. AND I WOULDN'T HAVE LET ANITA HERE JOIN AS EMPRESS IF I DIDN'T THINK YOU WERE TRUSTWORTHY.
THANKS, DADDY.
BUT THE APES' UPPER ECHELON IS STILL SUSPICIOUS OF YOU. IF YOU COOPERATE, IT WOULD CONSTITUTE SERIOUS FENCE MENDING.
WHAT DID YOU HAVE IN MIND?
"WE'RE PROPOSING THAT YOU, ROBIN... ALONG WITH EMPRESS, WONDER GIRL, AND SECRET, GO UNDER-COVER AT ROSENBERG. GET FRIENDLY WITH ALEX FLEMING, HIS CIVILIAN FRIEND BUTCH MOODY, AND HIS GALPALS, IF THEY'RE THERE. SEE IF YOU CAN DETERMINE WHETHER THEY DID BREAK INTO OUR HQ... AND WHAT, IF ANY-THING, THEY TOOK."
JULIUS ROSENBERG HIGH SCHOOL
"WHY JUST US FOUR?"
"BECAUSE SUPER-BOY MAY BE TOO RECOGNIZABLE, AND IMPULSE IS JUST TOO... IMPULSE."

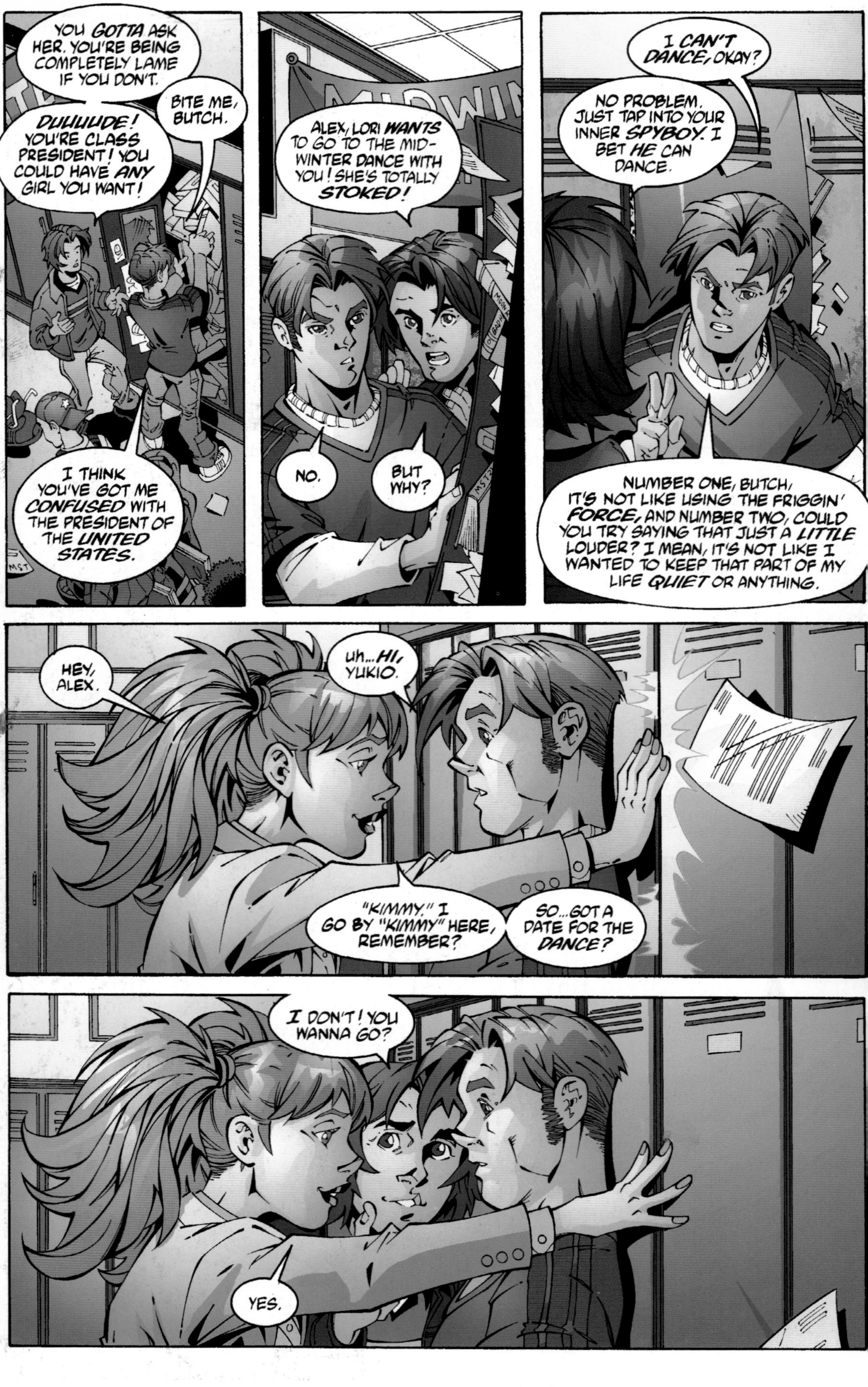
YOU *GOTTA* ASK HER. YOU'RE BEING COMPLETELY LAME IF YOU DON'T.
BITE ME, BUTCH.
DUUUUDE! YOU'RE CLASS PRESIDENT! YOU COULD HAVE *ANY* GIRL YOU WANT!
I THINK YOU'VE GOT ME *CONFUSED* WITH THE PRESIDENT OF THE *UNITED STATES.*
ALEX, LORI *WANTS* TO GO TO THE MID-WINTER DANCE WITH YOU! SHE'S TOTALLY *STOKED!*
NO.
BUT WHY?
I *CAN'T DANCE,* OKAY?
NO PROBLEM. JUST TAP INTO YOUR INNER *SPYBOY.* I BET *HE* CAN DANCE.
NUMBER ONE, BUTCH, IT'S NOT LIKE USING THE FRIGGIN' *FORCE,* AND NUMBER TWO, COULD YOU TRY SAYING THAT JUST A *LITTLE* LOUDER? I MEAN, IT'S NOT LIKE I WANTED TO KEEP THAT PART OF MY LIFE *QUIET* OR ANYTHING.
HEY, ALEX.
uh...*HI,* YUKIO.
"*KIMMY.*" I GO BY "*KIMMY*" HERE, REMEMBER?
SO...GOT A DATE FOR THE *DANCE?*
I DON'T! YOU WANNA GO?
YES.

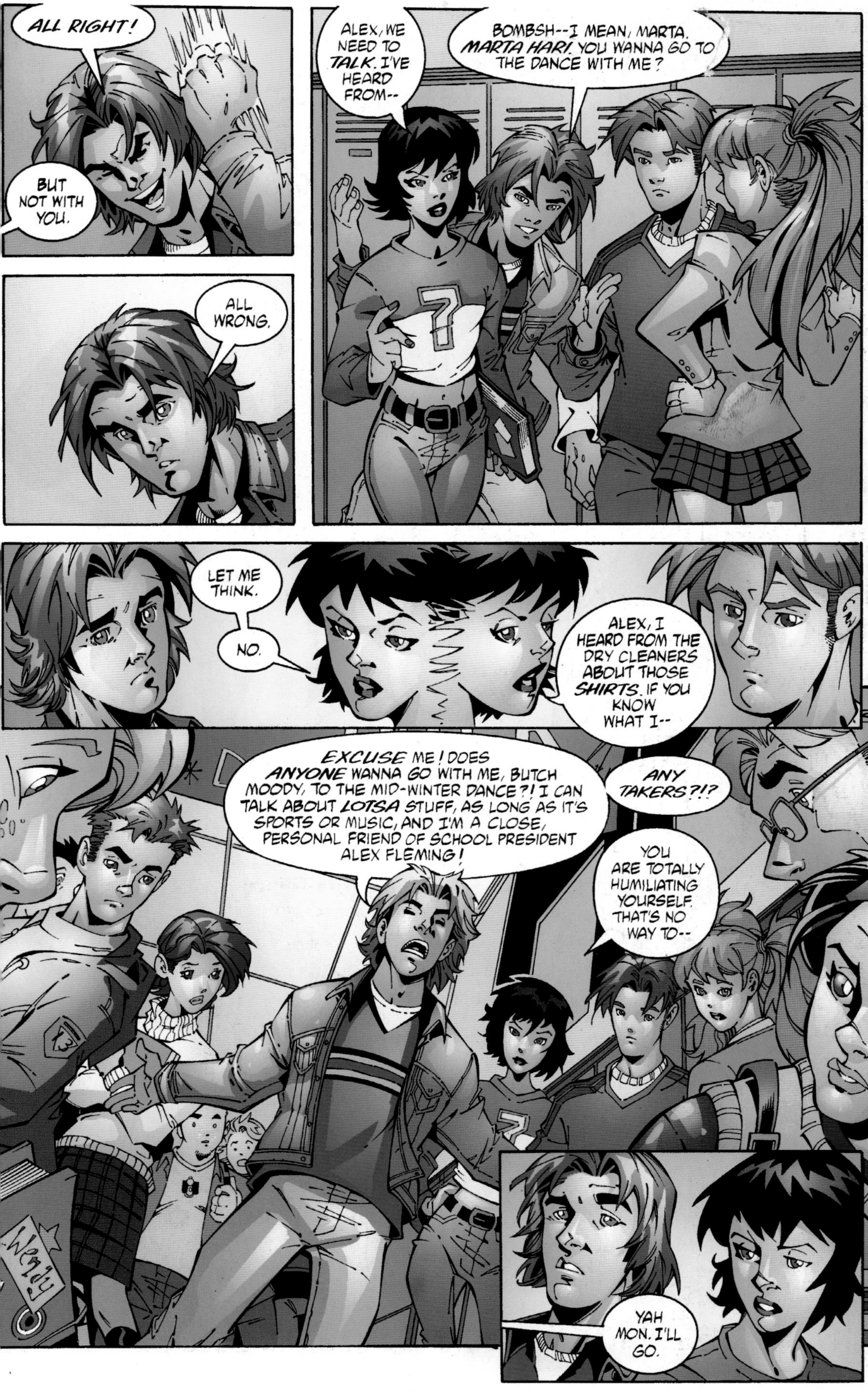
ALL RIGHT!
BUT NOT WITH YOU.
ALL WRONG.
ALEX, WE NEED TO TALK. I'VE HEARD FROM--
BOMBSH--I MEAN, MARTA. MARTA HARI. YOU WANNA GO TO THE DANCE WITH ME?
LET ME THINK.
NO.
ALEX, I HEARD FROM THE DRY CLEANERS ABOUT THOSE SHIRTS. IF YOU KNOW WHAT I--
EXCUSE ME! DOES ANYONE WANNA GO WITH ME, BUTCH MOODY, TO THE MID-WINTER DANCE?! I CAN TALK ABOUT LOTSA STUFF, AS LONG AS IT'S SPORTS OR MUSIC, AND I'M A CLOSE, PERSONAL FRIEND OF SCHOOL PRESIDENT ALEX FLEMING!
ANY TAKERS?!?
YOU ARE TOTALLY HUMILIATING YOURSELF. THAT'S NO WAY TO--
YAH MON. I'LL GO.

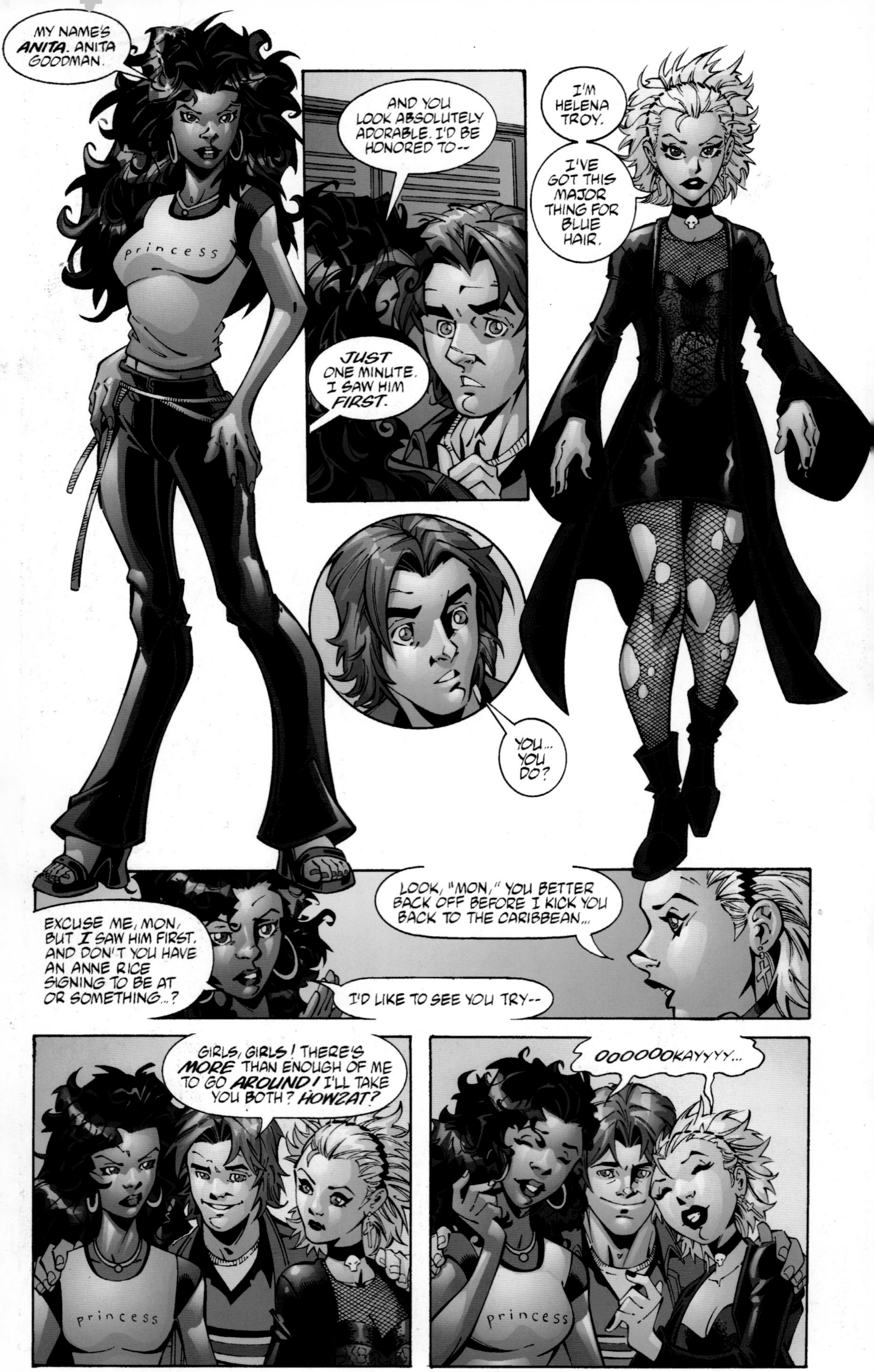
MY NAME'S ANITA. ANITA GOODMAN.
AND YOU LOOK ABSOLUTELY ADORABLE. I'D BE HONORED TO--
JUST ONE MINUTE. I SAW HIM FIRST.
I'M HELENA TROY.
I'VE GOT THIS MAJOR THING FOR BLUE HAIR.
YOU... YOU DO?
EXCUSE ME, MON, BUT I SAW HIM FIRST. AND DON'T YOU HAVE AN ANNE RICE SIGNING TO BE AT OR SOMETHING...?
LOOK, "MON," YOU BETTER BACK OFF BEFORE I KICK YOU BACK TO THE CARIBBEAN...
I'D LIKE TO SEE YOU TRY--
GIRLS, GIRLS! THERE'S MORE THAN ENOUGH OF ME TO GO AROUND! I'LL TAKE YOU BOTH? HOWZAT?
OOOOOOKAYYYY...

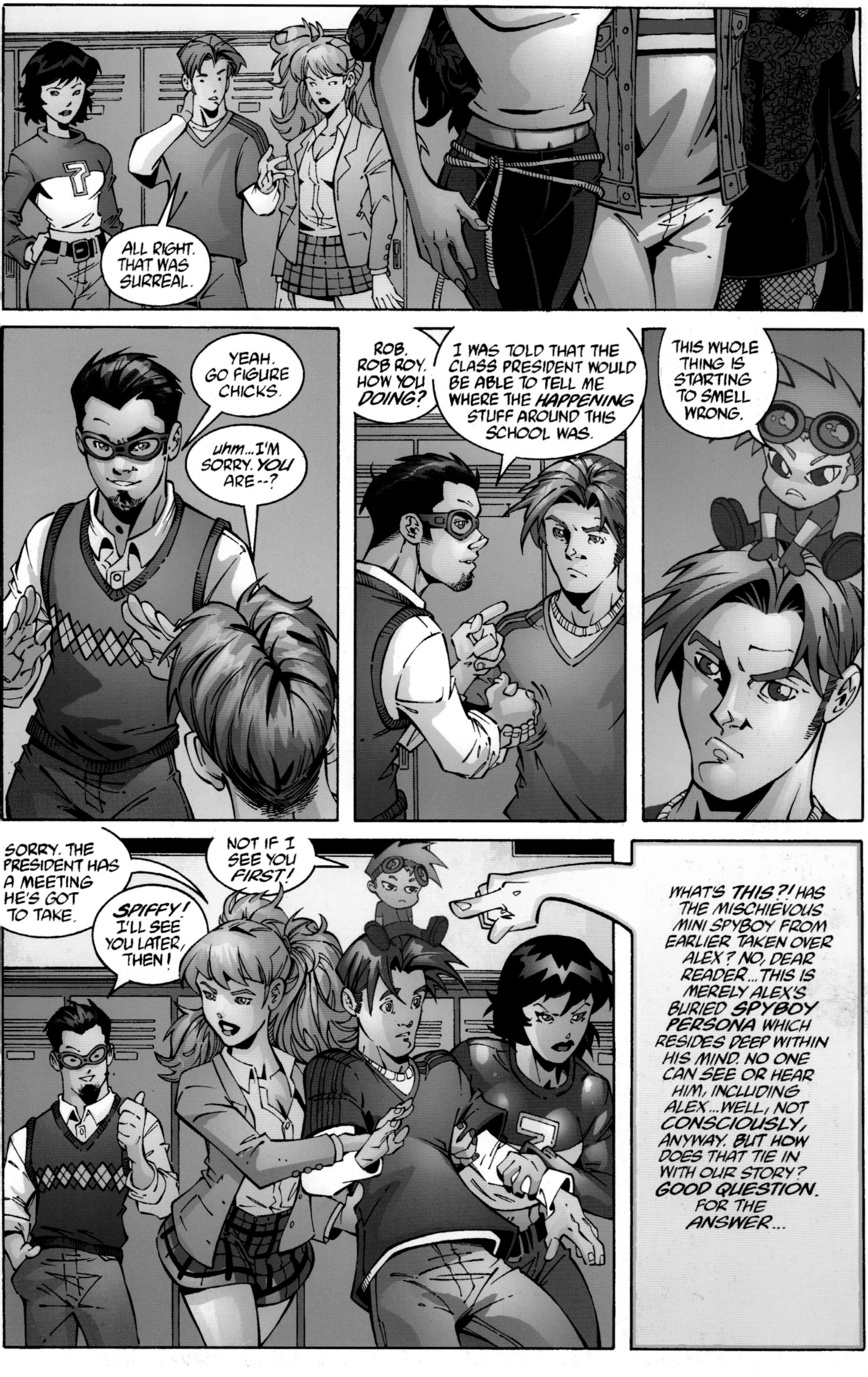

ALL RIGHT. THAT WAS SURREAL.
YEAH. GO FIGURE CHICKS.
uhm... I'M SORRY. YOU ARE--?
ROB. ROB ROY. HOW YOU DOING?
I WAS TOLD THAT THE CLASS PRESIDENT WOULD BE ABLE TO TELL ME WHERE THE HAPPENING STUFF AROUND THIS SCHOOL WAS.
THIS WHOLE THING IS STARTING TO SMELL WRONG.
SORRY. THE PRESIDENT HAS A MEETING HE'S GOT TO TAKE.
SPIFFY! I'LL SEE YOU LATER, THEN!
NOT IF I SEE YOU FIRST!
WHAT'S THIS?! HAS THE MISCHIEVOUS MINI SPYBOY FROM EARLIER TAKEN OVER ALEX? NO, DEAR READER... THIS IS MERELY ALEX'S BURIED SPYBOY PERSONA WHICH RESIDES DEEP WITHIN HIS MIND. NO ONE CAN SEE OR HEAR HIM, INCLUDING ALEX... WELL, NOT CONSCIOUSLY, ANYWAY. BUT HOW DOES THAT TIE IN WITH OUR STORY? GOOD QUESTION. FOR THE ANSWER...

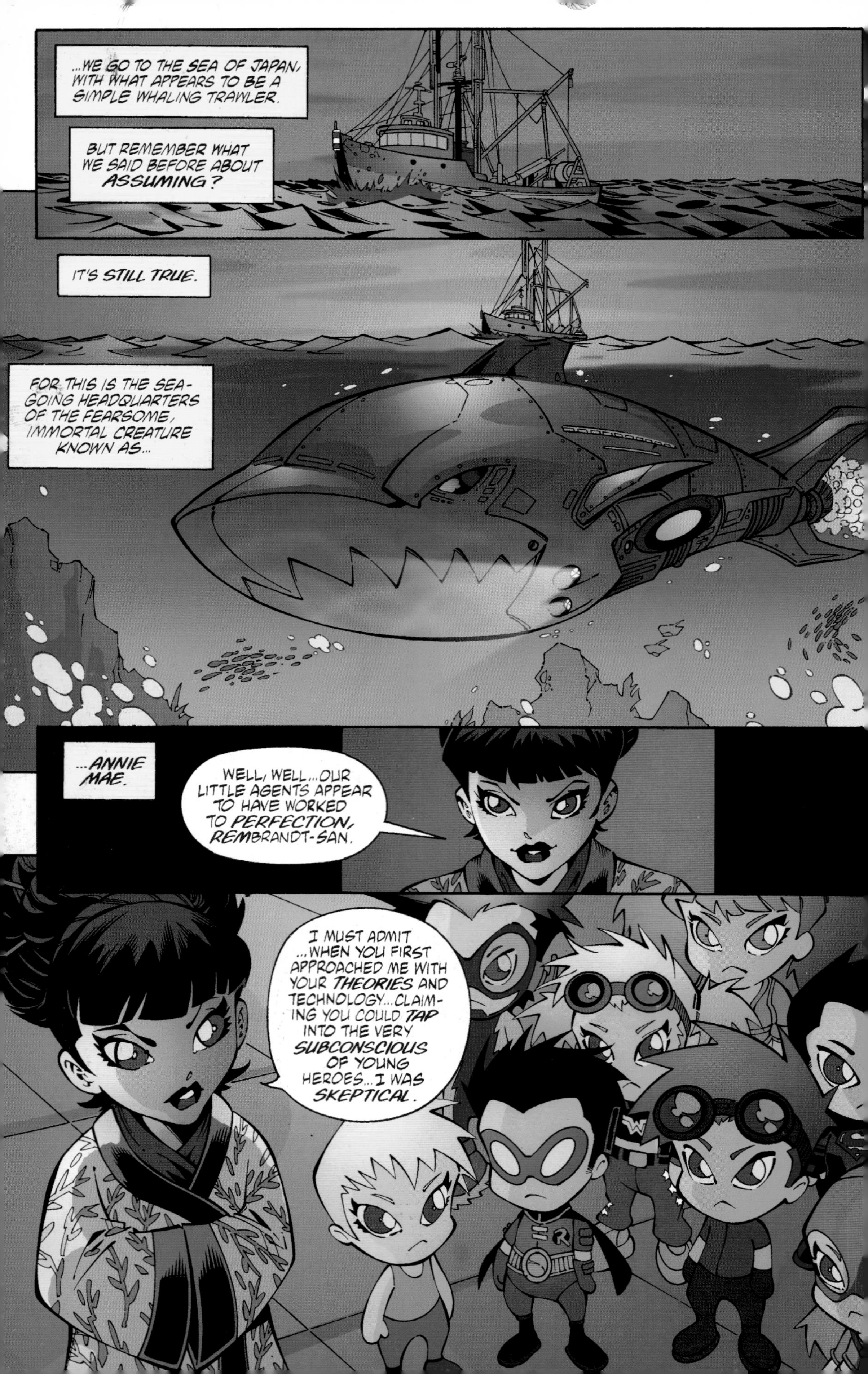
...WE GO TO THE SEA OF JAPAN, WITH WHAT APPEARS TO BE A SIMPLE WHALING TRAWLER.
BUT REMEMBER WHAT WE SAID BEFORE ABOUT ASSUMING?
IT'S STILL TRUE.
FOR THIS IS THE SEA-GOING HEADQUARTERS OF THE FEARSOME, IMMORTAL CREATURE KNOWN AS...
...ANNIE MAE.
WELL, WELL...OUR LITTLE AGENTS APPEAR TO HAVE WORKED TO PERFECTION, REMBRANDT-SAN.
I MUST ADMIT ...WHEN YOU FIRST APPROACHED ME WITH YOUR THEORIES AND TECHNOLOGY...CLAIMING YOU COULD TAP INTO THE VERY SUBCONSCIOUS OF YOUNG HEROES...I WAS SKEPTICAL.

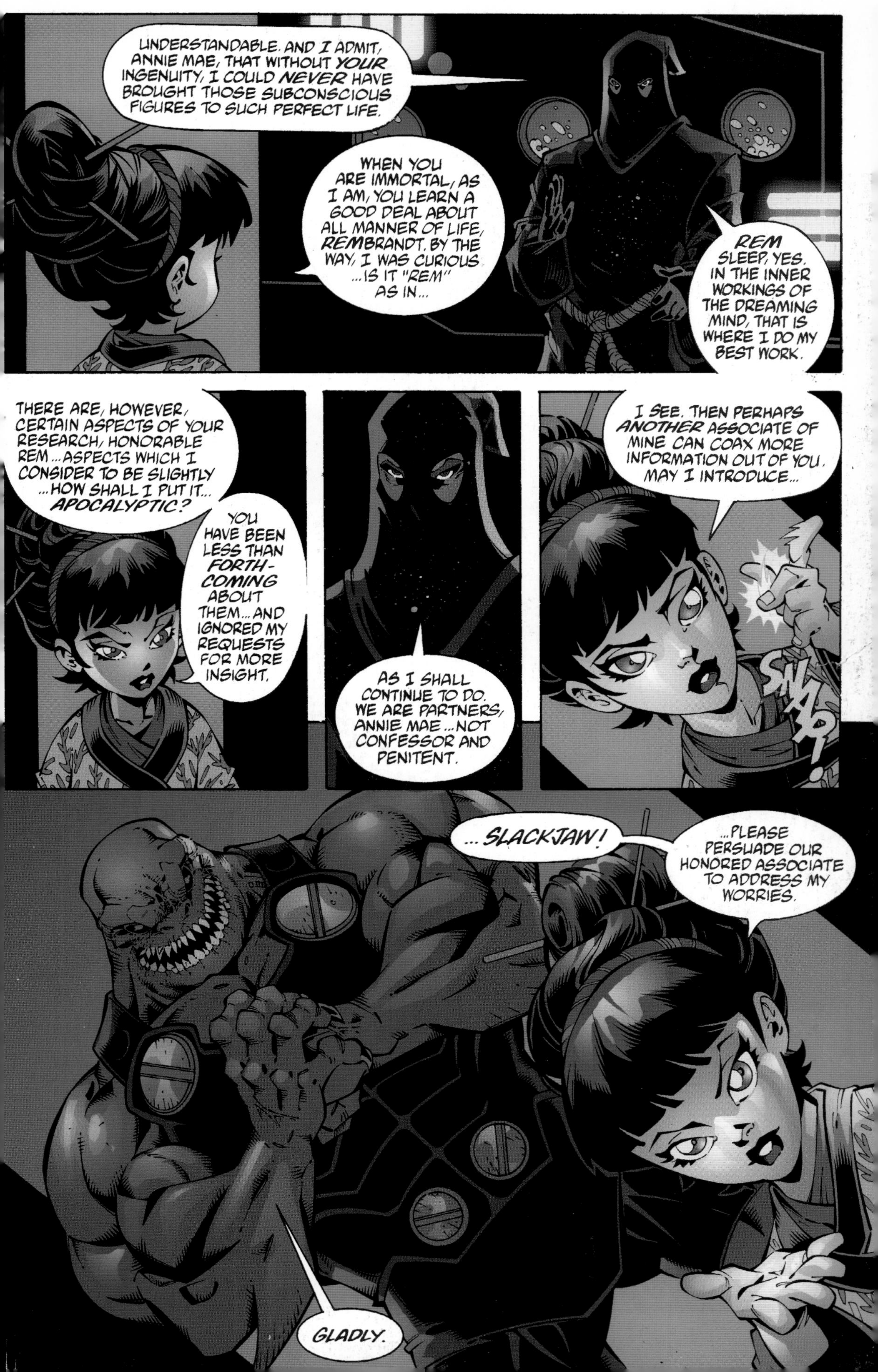
UNDERSTANDABLE. AND I ADMIT, ANNIE MAE, THAT WITHOUT YOUR INGENUITY, I COULD NEVER HAVE BROUGHT THOSE SUBCONSCIOUS FIGURES TO SUCH PERFECT LIFE.
WHEN YOU ARE IMMORTAL, AS I AM, YOU LEARN A GOOD DEAL ABOUT ALL MANNER OF LIFE, REMBRANDT. BY THE WAY, I WAS CURIOUS ...IS IT "REM" AS IN...
REM SLEEP, YES. IN THE INNER WORKINGS OF THE DREAMING MIND, THAT IS WHERE I DO MY BEST WORK.
THERE ARE, HOWEVER, CERTAIN ASPECTS OF YOUR RESEARCH, HONORABLE REM ...ASPECTS WHICH I CONSIDER TO BE SLIGHTLY ...HOW SHALL I PUT IT... APOCALYPTIC?
YOU HAVE BEEN LESS THAN FORTH-COMING ABOUT THEM... AND IGNORED MY REQUESTS FOR MORE INSIGHT.
AS I SHALL CONTINUE TO DO. WE ARE PARTNERS, ANNIE MAE ...NOT CONFESSOR AND PENITENT.
I SEE. THEN PERHAPS ANOTHER ASSOCIATE OF MINE CAN COAX MORE INFORMATION OUT OF YOU. MAY I INTRODUCE...
SNAP!
...SLACKJAW!
...PLEASE PERSUADE OUR HONORED ASSOCIATE TO ADDRESS MY WORRIES.
GLADLY.

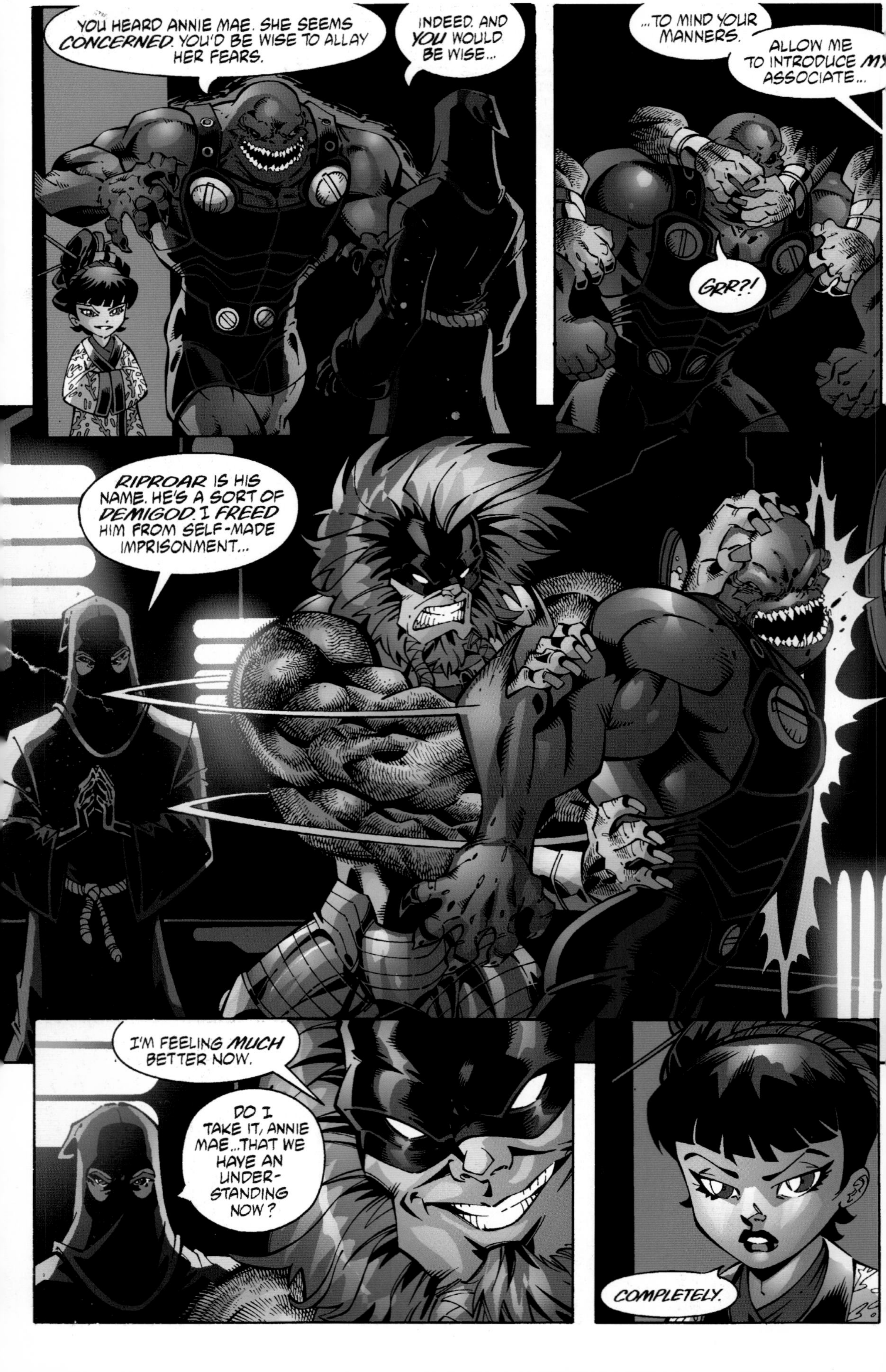
YOU HEARD ANNIE MAE. SHE SEEMS CONCERNED. YOU'D BE WISE TO ALLAY HER FEARS.
INDEED. AND YOU WOULD BE WISE...
...TO MIND YOUR MANNERS.
ALLOW ME TO INTRODUCE MY ASSOCIATE...
GRR?!
RIPROAR IS HIS NAME. HE'S A SORT OF DEMIGOD. I FREED HIM FROM SELF-MADE IMPRISONMENT...
I'M FEELING MUCH BETTER NOW.
DO I TAKE IT, ANNIE MAE...THAT WE HAVE AN UNDER-STANDING NOW?
COMPLETELY.

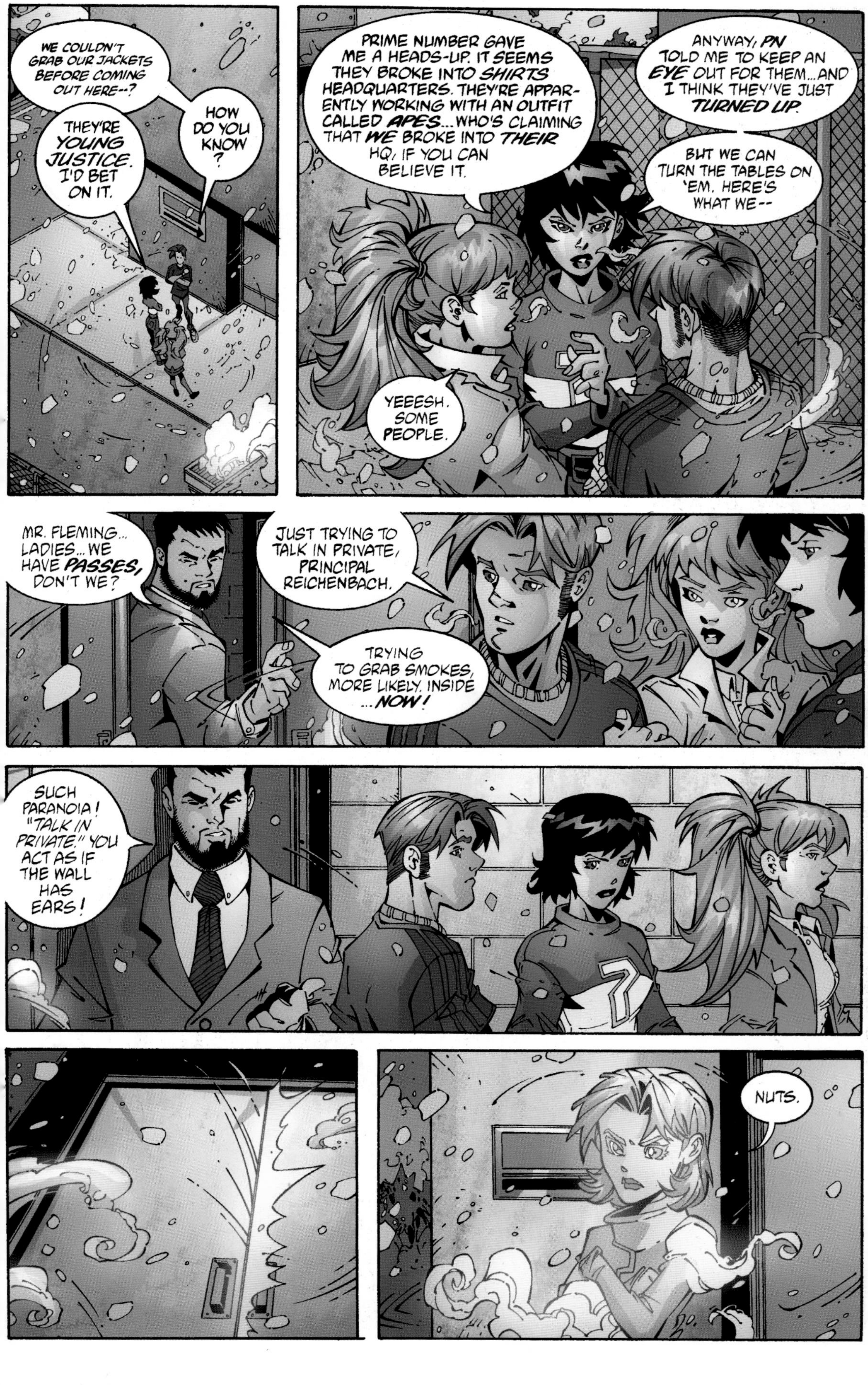
WE COULDN'T GRAB OUR JACKETS BEFORE COMING OUT HERE--?
THEY'RE YOUNG JUSTICE. I'D BET ON IT.
HOW DO YOU KNOW?
PRIME NUMBER GAVE ME A HEADS-UP. IT SEEMS THEY BROKE INTO SHIRTS HEADQUARTERS. THEY'RE APPARENTLY WORKING WITH AN OUTFIT CALLED APES... WHO'S CLAIMING THAT WE BROKE INTO THEIR HQ, IF YOU CAN BELIEVE IT.
ANYWAY, PN TOLD ME TO KEEP AN EYE OUT FOR THEM... AND I THINK THEY'VE JUST TURNED UP.
BUT WE CAN TURN THE TABLES ON 'EM. HERE'S WHAT WE--
YEEEESH. SOME PEOPLE.
MR. FLEMING... LADIES... WE HAVE PASSES, DON'T WE?
JUST TRYING TO TALK IN PRIVATE, PRINCIPAL REICHENBACH.
TRYING TO GRAB SMOKES, MORE LIKELY. INSIDE ...NOW!
SUCH PARANOIA! "TALK IN PRIVATE." YOU ACT AS IF THE WALL HAS EARS!
NUTS.

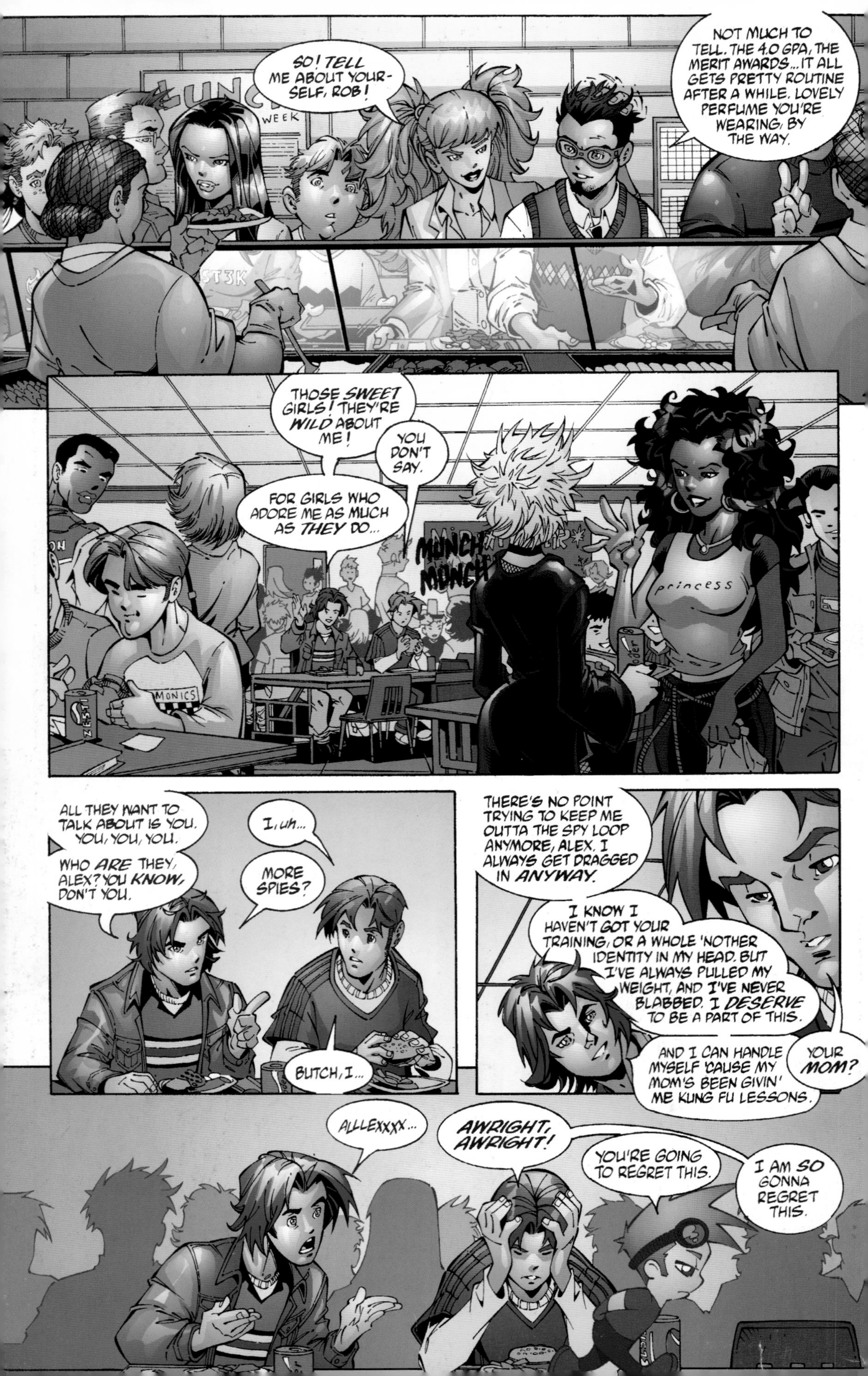
SO! TELL ME ABOUT YOUR-SELF, ROB!
NOT MUCH TO TELL. THE 4.0 GPA, THE MERIT AWARDS... IT ALL GETS PRETTY ROUTINE AFTER A WHILE. LOVELY PERFUME YOU'RE WEARING, BY THE WAY.
THOSE SWEET GIRLS! THEY'RE WILD ABOUT ME!
YOU DON'T SAY.
FOR GIRLS WHO ADORE ME AS MUCH AS THEY DO...
MUNCH MUNCH
princess
ALL THEY WANT TO TALK ABOUT IS YOU. YOU, YOU, YOU.
I, uh...
WHO ARE THEY, ALEX? YOU KNOW, DON'T YOU.
MORE SPIES?
BUTCH, I...
THERE'S NO POINT TRYING TO KEEP ME OUTTA THE SPY LOOP ANYMORE, ALEX. I ALWAYS GET DRAGGED IN ANYWAY.
I KNOW I HAVEN'T GOT YOUR TRAINING, OR A WHOLE 'NOTHER IDENTITY IN MY HEAD. BUT I'VE ALWAYS PULLED MY WEIGHT, AND I'VE NEVER BLABBED. I DESERVE TO BE A PART OF THIS.
AND I CAN HANDLE MYSELF 'CAUSE MY MOM'S BEEN GIVIN' ME KUNG FU LESSONS.
YOUR MOM?
ALLLEXXXX...
AWRIGHT, AWRIGHT!
YOU'RE GOING TO REGRET THIS.
I AM SO GONNA REGRET THIS.

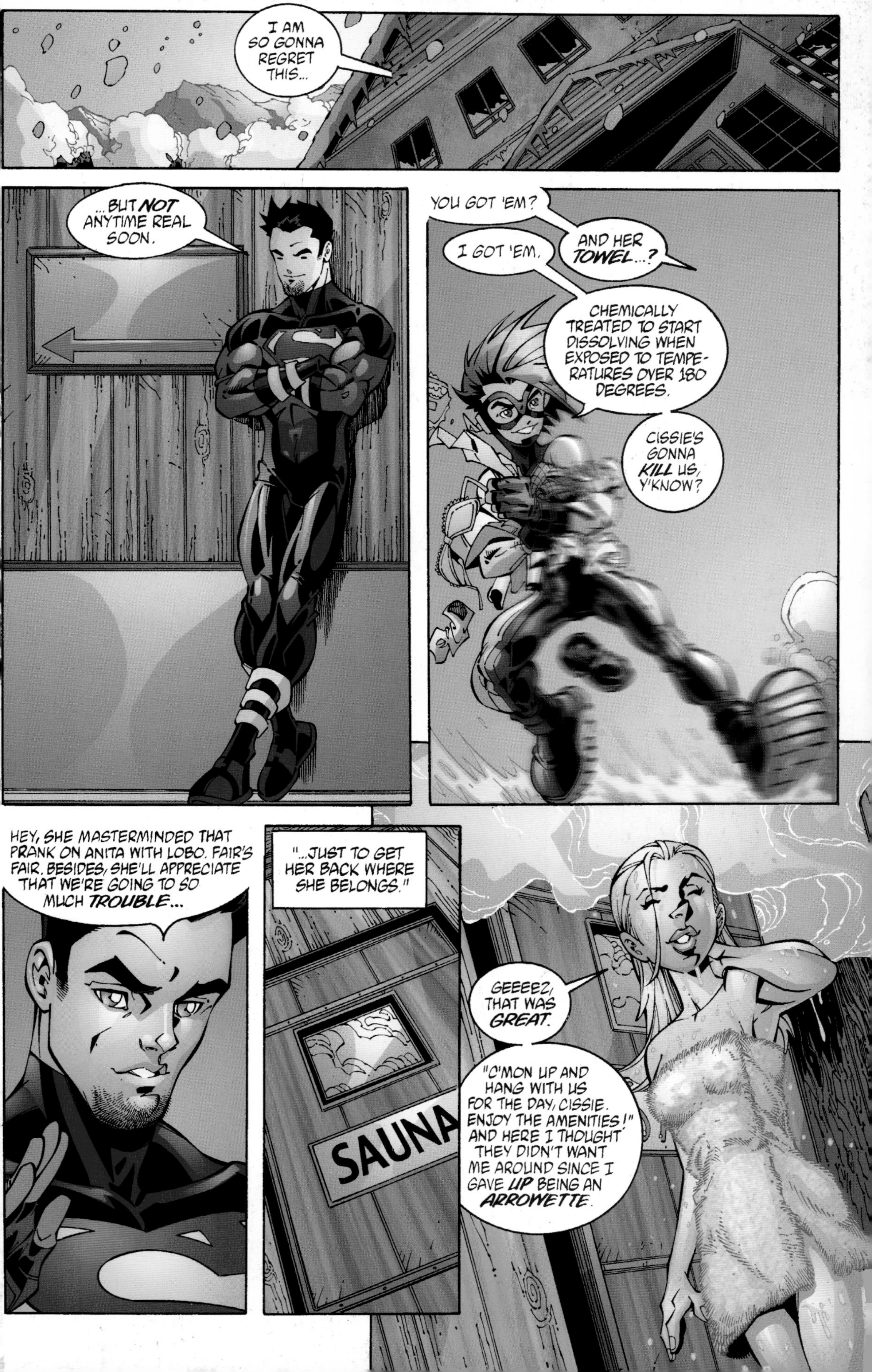
I AM SO GONNA REGRET THIS...
...BUT NOT ANYTIME REAL SOON.
YOU GOT 'EM?
I GOT 'EM.
AND HER TOWEL...?
CHEMICALLY TREATED TO START DISSOLVING WHEN EXPOSED TO TEMPERATURES OVER 180 DEGREES.
CISSIE'S GONNA KILL US, Y'KNOW?
HEY, SHE MASTERMINDED THAT PRANK ON ANITA WITH LOBO. FAIR'S FAIR. BESIDES, SHE'LL APPRECIATE THAT WE'RE GOING TO SO MUCH TROUBLE...
"...JUST TO GET HER BACK WHERE SHE BELONGS."
SAUNA
GEEEEZ, THAT WAS GREAT.
"C'MON UP AND HANG WITH US FOR THE DAY, CISSIE. ENJOY THE AMENITIES!" AND HERE I THOUGHT THEY DIDN'T WANT ME AROUND SINCE I GAVE UP BEING AN ARROWETTE.

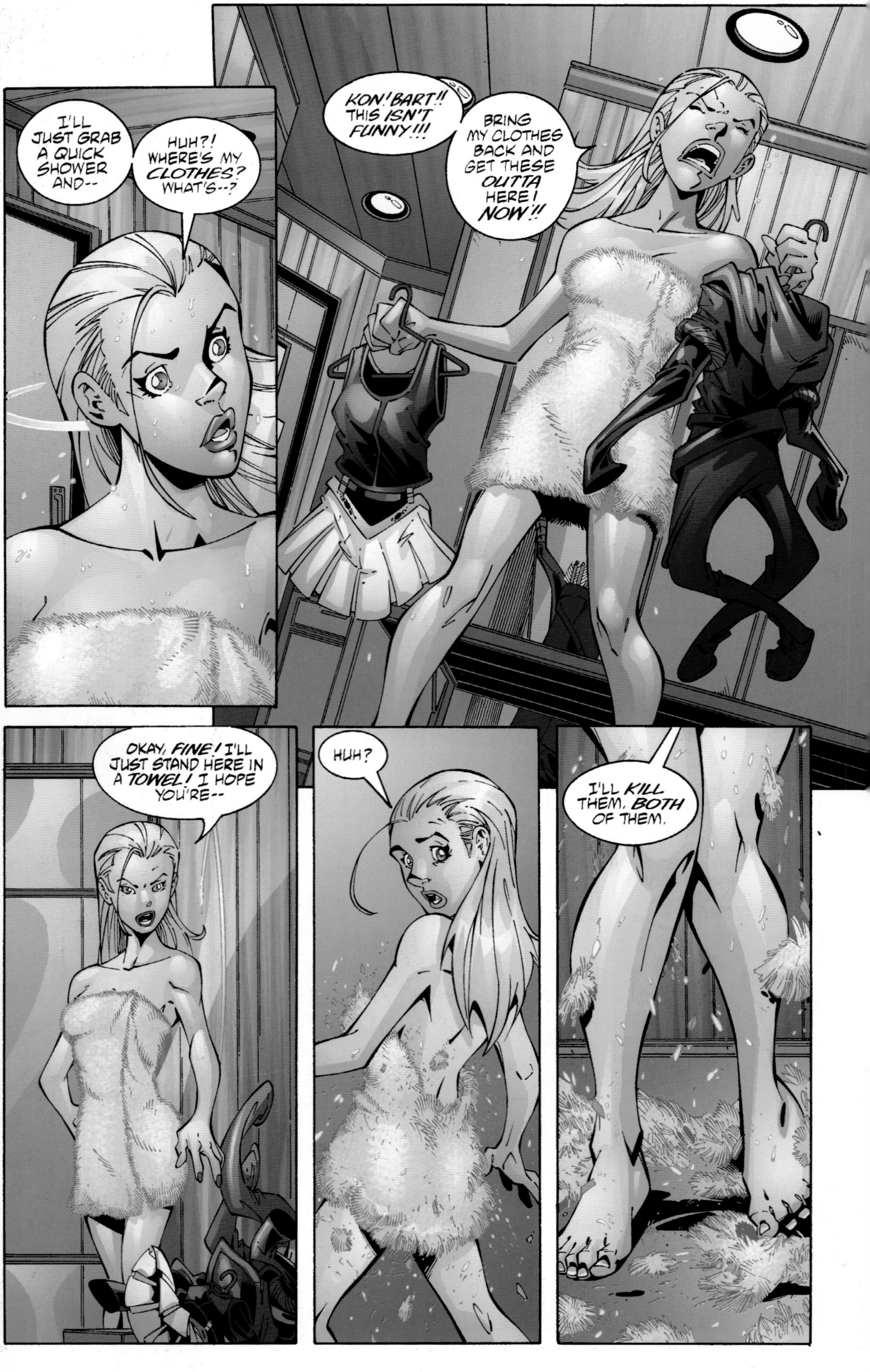
I'LL JUST GRAB A QUICK SHOWER AND--
HUH?! WHERE'S MY CLOTHES? WHAT'S--?
KON! BART!! THIS ISN'T FUNNY!!!
BRING MY CLOTHES BACK AND GET THESE OUTTA HERE! NOW!!
OKAY, FINE! I'LL JUST STAND HERE IN A TOWEL! I HOPE YOU'RE--
HUH?
I'LL KILL THEM. BOTH OF THEM.

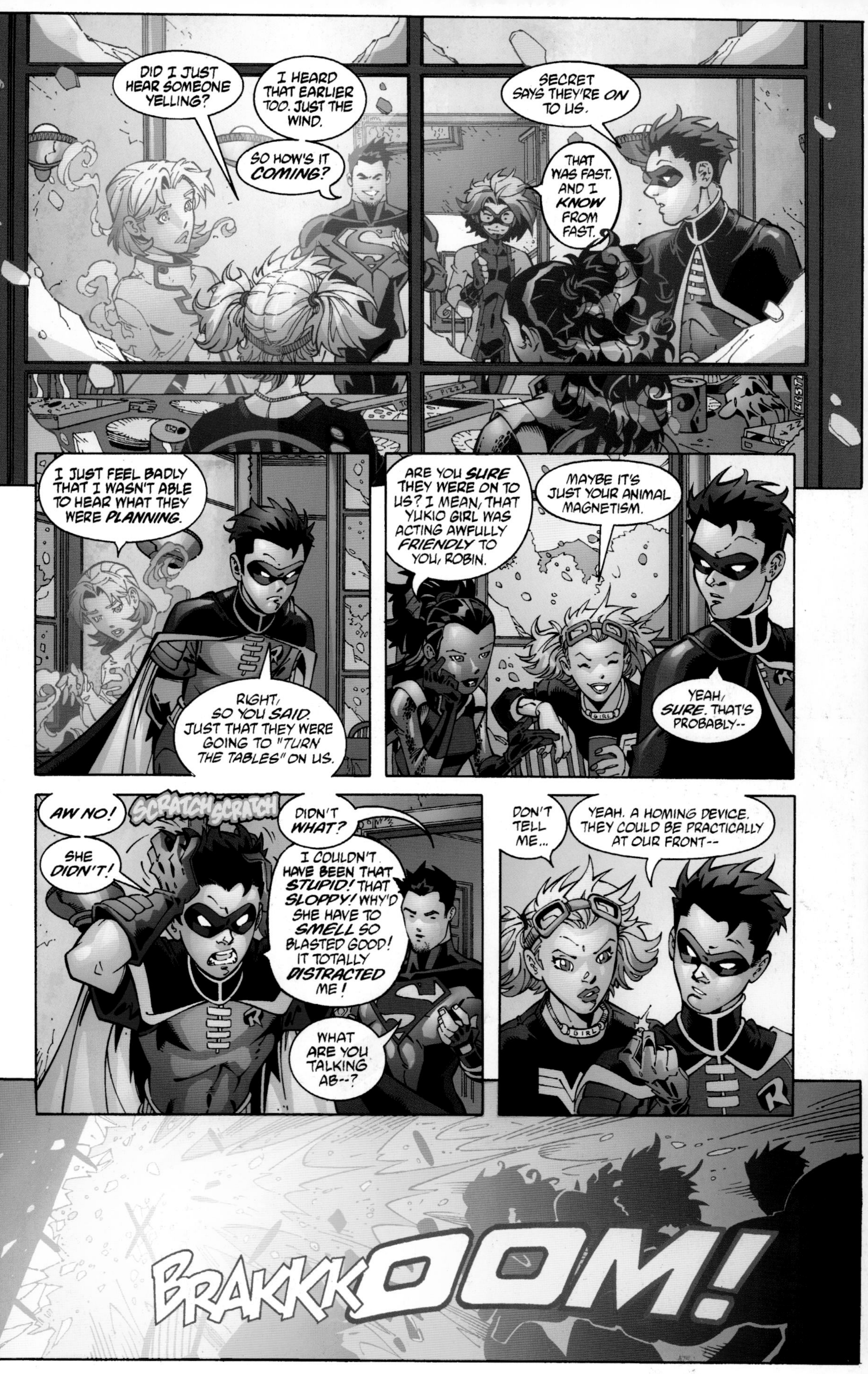
DID I JUST HEAR SOMEONE YELLING?
I HEARD THAT EARLIER TOO. JUST THE WIND.
SO HOW'S IT COMING?
SECRET SAYS THEY'RE ON TO US.
THAT WAS FAST. AND I KNOW FROM FAST.
I JUST FEEL BADLY THAT I WASN'T ABLE TO HEAR WHAT THEY WERE PLANNING.
RIGHT, SO YOU SAID. JUST THAT THEY WERE GOING TO "TURN THE TABLES" ON US.
ARE YOU SURE THEY WERE ON TO US? I MEAN, THAT YUKIO GIRL WAS ACTING AWFULLY FRIENDLY TO YOU, ROBIN.
MAYBE IT'S JUST YOUR ANIMAL MAGNETISM.
YEAH, SURE. THAT'S PROBABLY--
AW NO!
SCRATCH SCRATCH
SHE DIDN'T!
DIDN'T WHAT?
I COULDN'T HAVE BEEN THAT STUPID! THAT SLOPPY! WHY'D SHE HAVE TO SMELL SO BLASTED GOOD! IT TOTALLY DISTRACTED ME!
WHAT ARE YOU TALKING AB--?
DON'T TELL ME...
YEAH. A HOMING DEVICE. THEY COULD BE PRACTICALLY AT OUR FRONT--
BRAKKKOOM!

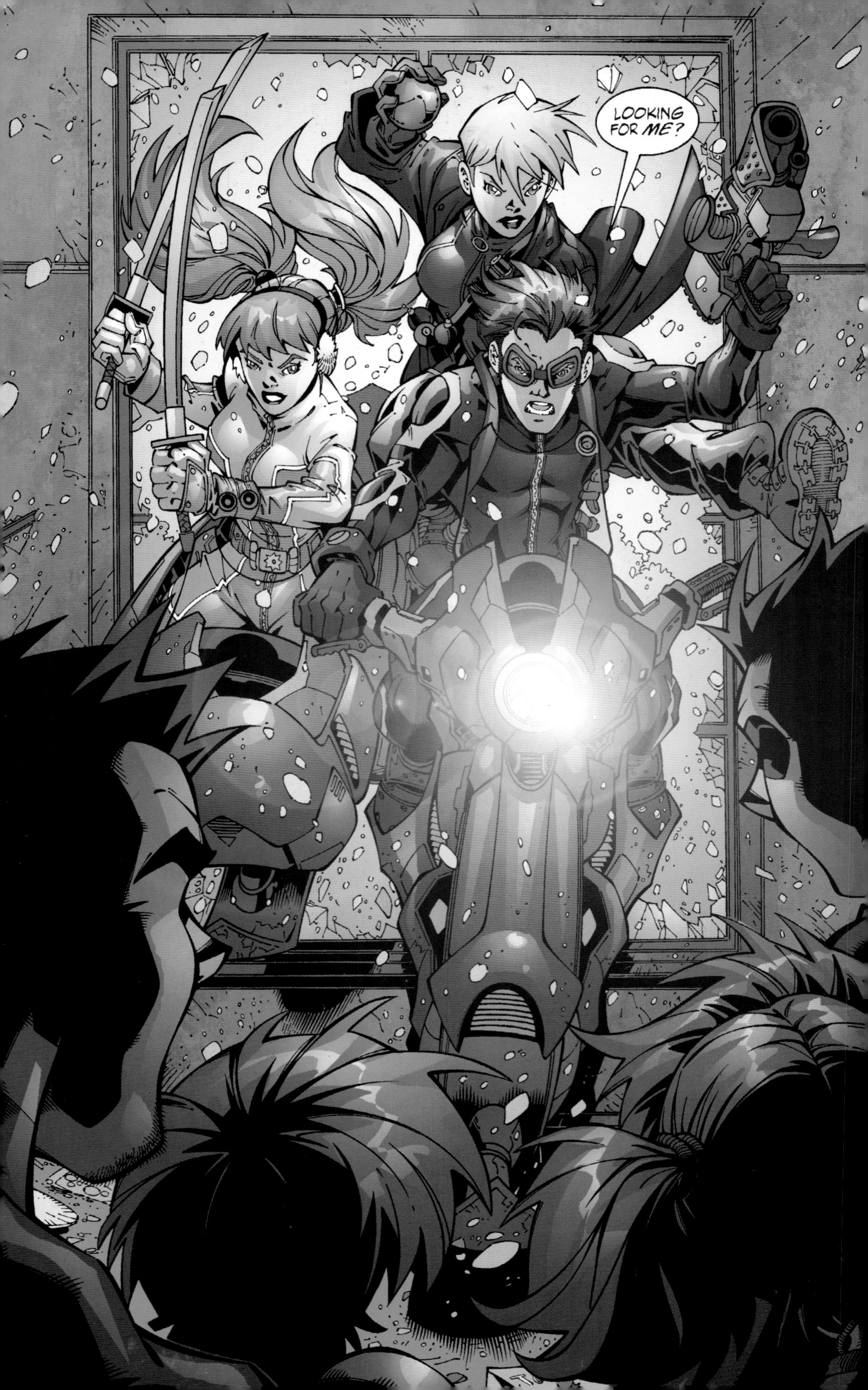
LOOKING FOR *ME*?

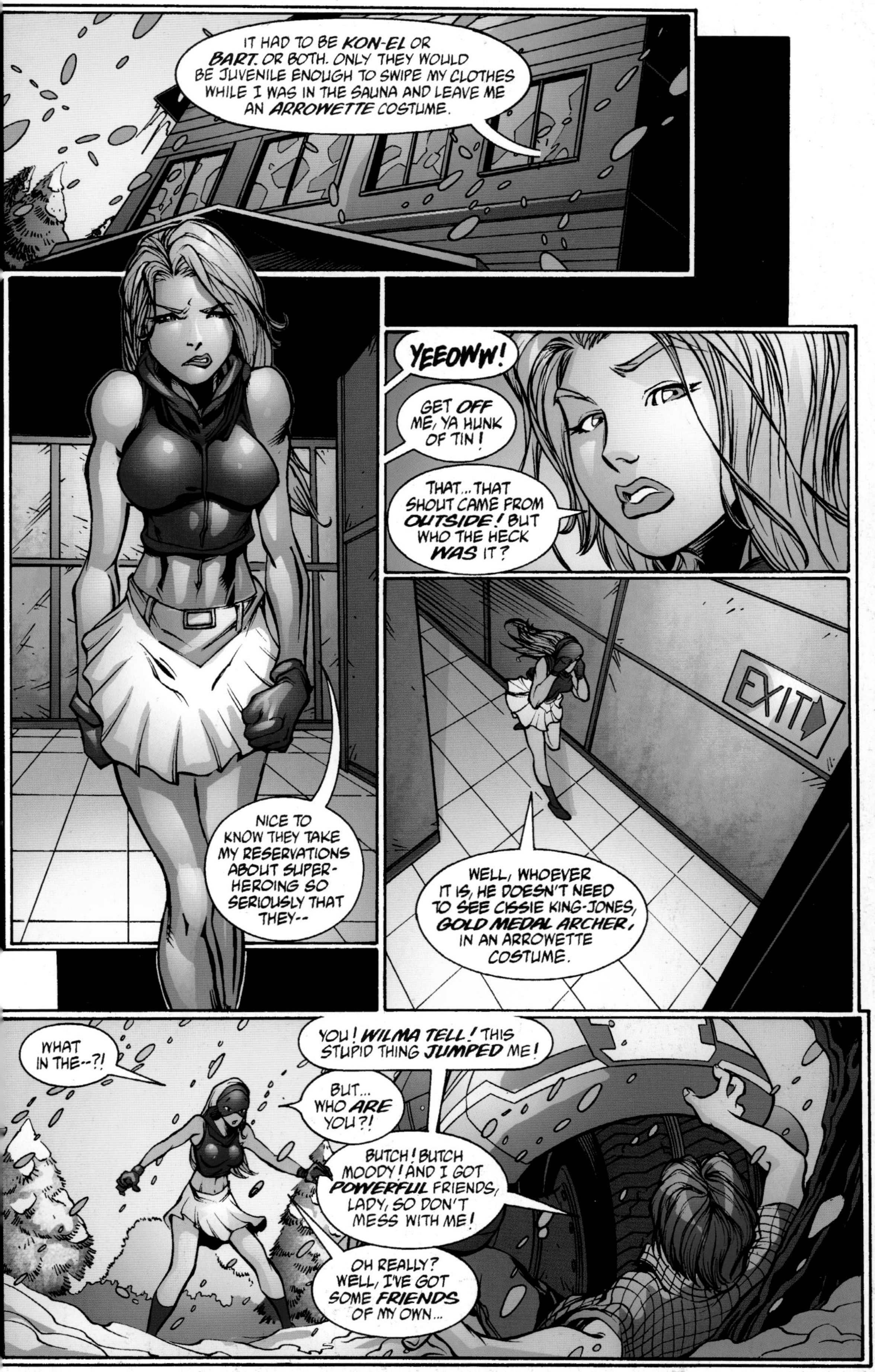
IT HAD TO BE KON-EL OR BART. OR BOTH. ONLY THEY WOULD BE JUVENILE ENOUGH TO SWIPE MY CLOTHES WHILE I WAS IN THE SAUNA AND LEAVE ME AN ARROWETTE COSTUME.
NICE TO KNOW THEY TAKE MY RESERVATIONS ABOUT SUPER-HEROING SO SERIOUSLY THAT THEY--
YEEOWW!
GET OFF ME, YA HUNK OF TIN!
THAT... THAT SHOUT CAME FROM OUTSIDE! BUT WHO THE HECK WAS IT?
EXIT
WELL, WHOEVER IT IS, HE DOESN'T NEED TO SEE CISSIE KING-JONES, GOLD MEDAL ARCHER, IN AN ARROWETTE COSTUME.
WHAT IN THE--?!
YOU! WILMA TELL! THIS STUPID THING JUMPED ME!
BUT... WHO ARE YOU?!
BUTCH! BUTCH MOODY! AND I GOT POWERFUL FRIENDS, LADY, SO DON'T MESS WITH ME!
OH REALLY? WELL, I'VE GOT SOME FRIENDS OF MY OWN...

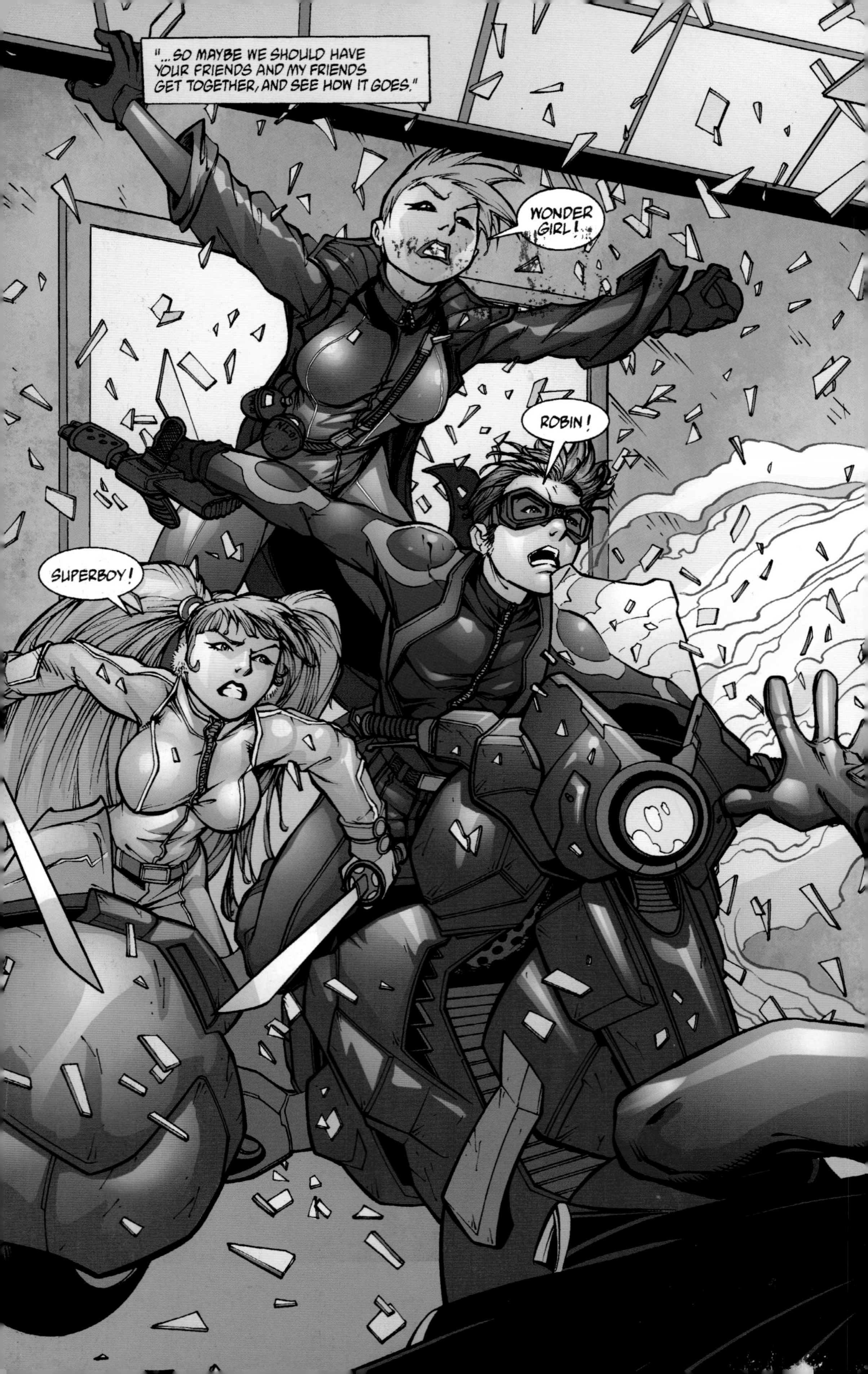
"...SO MAYBE WE SHOULD HAVE YOUR FRIENDS AND MY FRIENDS GET TOGETHER, AND SEE HOW IT GOES."
WONDER GIRL!
ROBIN!
SUPERBOY!

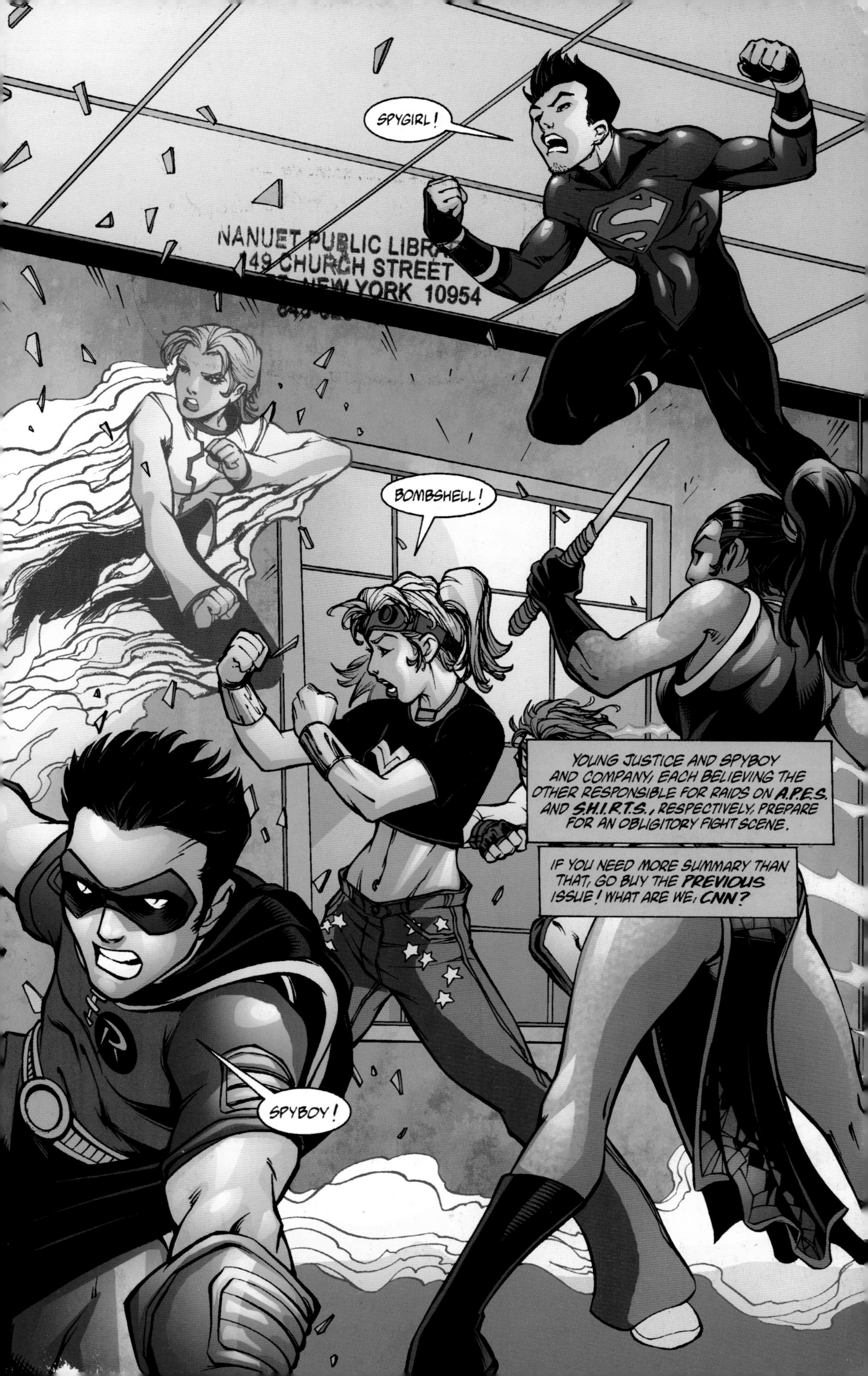
SPYGIRL!
BOMBSHELL!
YOUNG JUSTICE AND SPYBOY AND COMPANY, EACH BELIEVING THE OTHER RESPONSIBLE FOR RAIDS ON **A.P.E.S.** AND **S.H.I.R.T.S.**, RESPECTIVELY, PREPARE FOR AN OBLIGITORY FIGHT SCENE.
IF YOU NEED MORE SUMMARY THAN THAT, GO BUY THE **PREVIOUS** ISSUE! WHAT ARE WE, **CNN?**
SPYBOY!

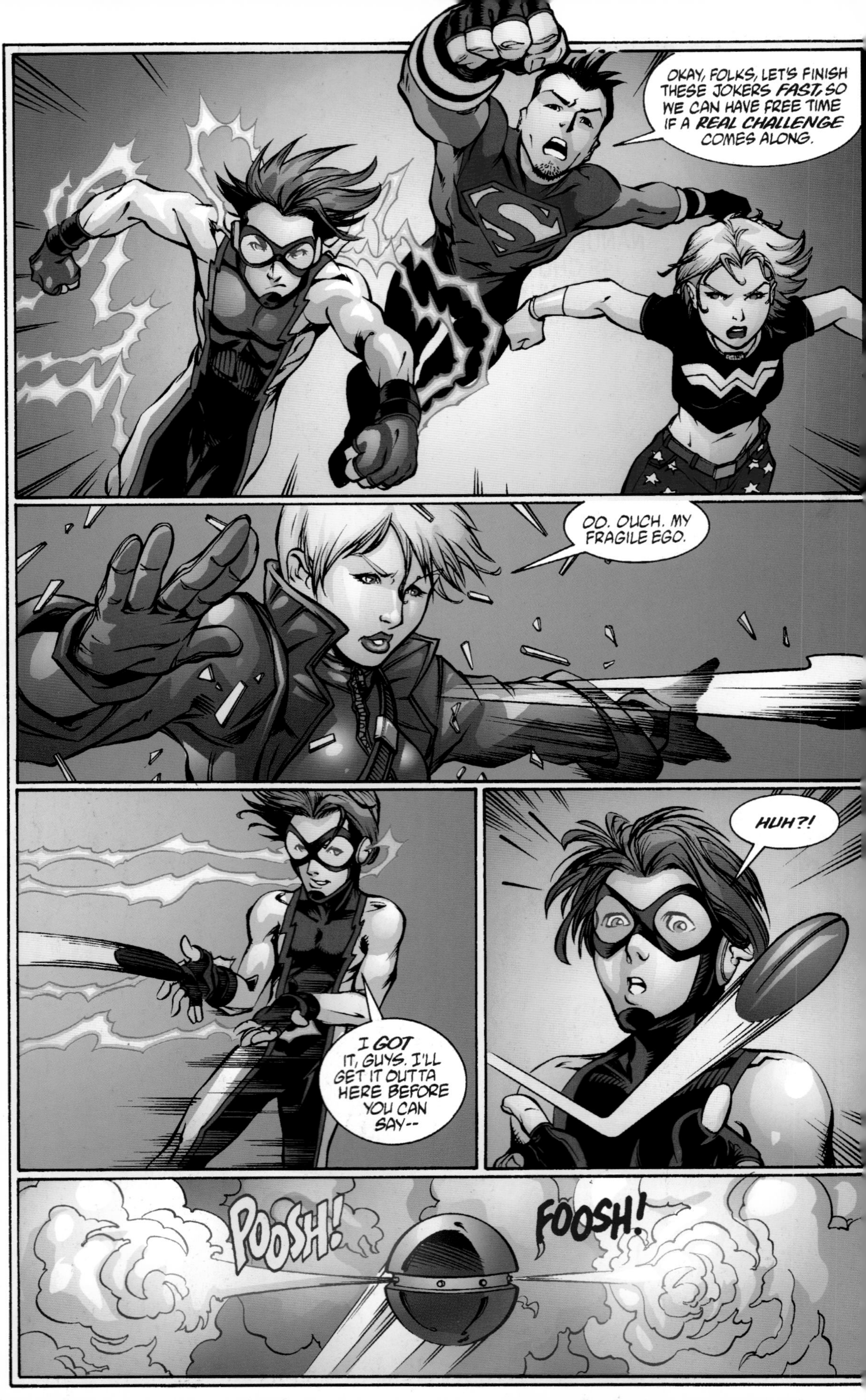

OKAY, FOLKS, LET'S FINISH THESE JOKERS FAST, SO WE CAN HAVE FREE TIME IF A REAL CHALLENGE COMES ALONG.
OO. OUCH. MY FRAGILE EGO.
I GOT IT, GUYS. I'LL GET IT OUTTA HERE BEFORE YOU CAN SAY--
HUH?!
POOSH!
FOOSH!

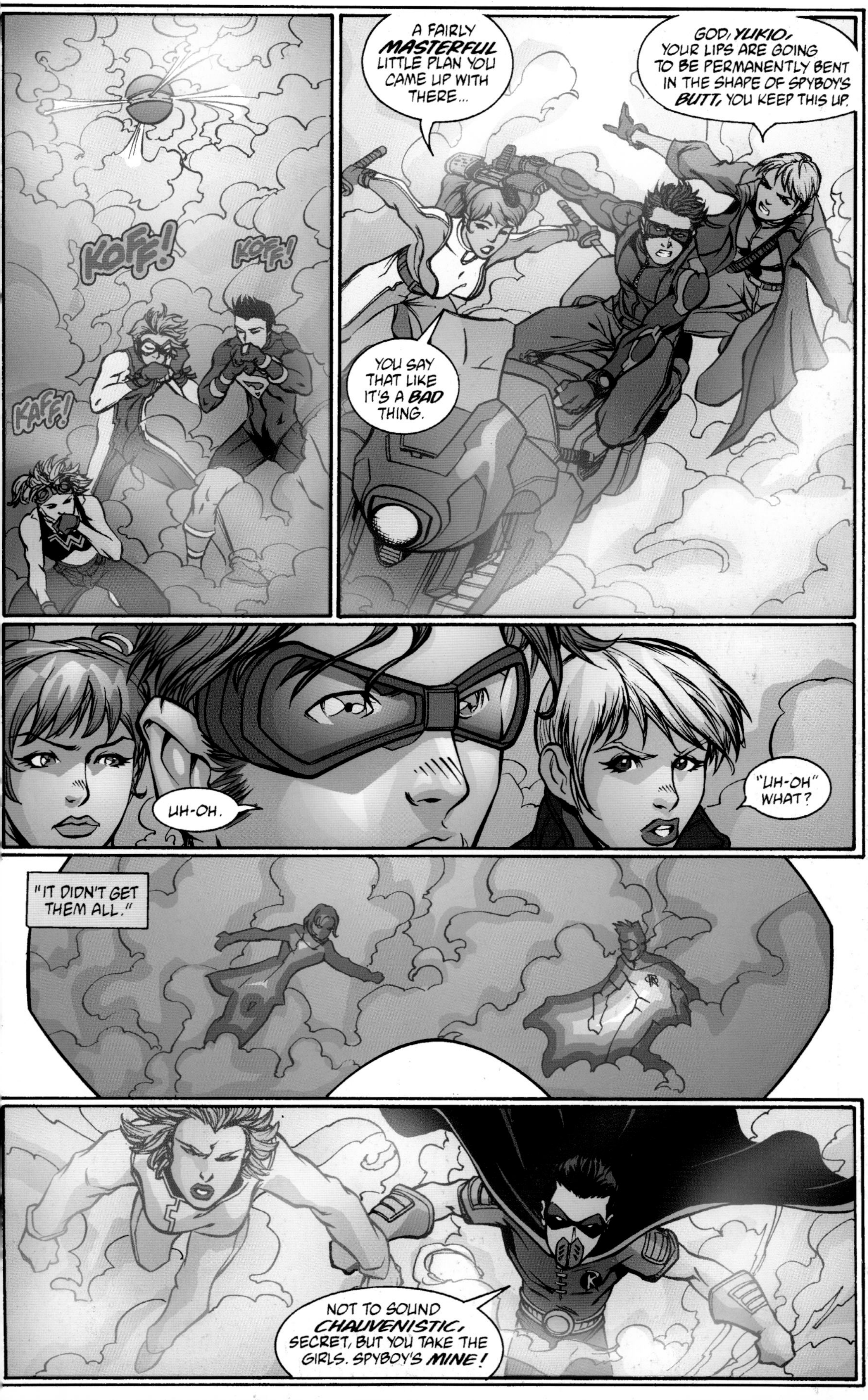
KOFF!
KOFF!
KAFF!
A FAIRLY MASTERFUL LITTLE PLAN YOU CAME UP WITH THERE...
GOD, YUKIO, YOUR LIPS ARE GOING TO BE PERMANENTLY BENT IN THE SHAPE OF SPYBOY'S BUTT, YOU KEEP THIS UP.
YOU SAY THAT LIKE IT'S A BAD THING.
UH-OH.
"UH-OH" WHAT?
"IT DIDN'T GET THEM ALL."
NOT TO SOUND CHAUVENISTIC, SECRET, BUT YOU TAKE THE GIRLS. SPYBOY'S MINE!

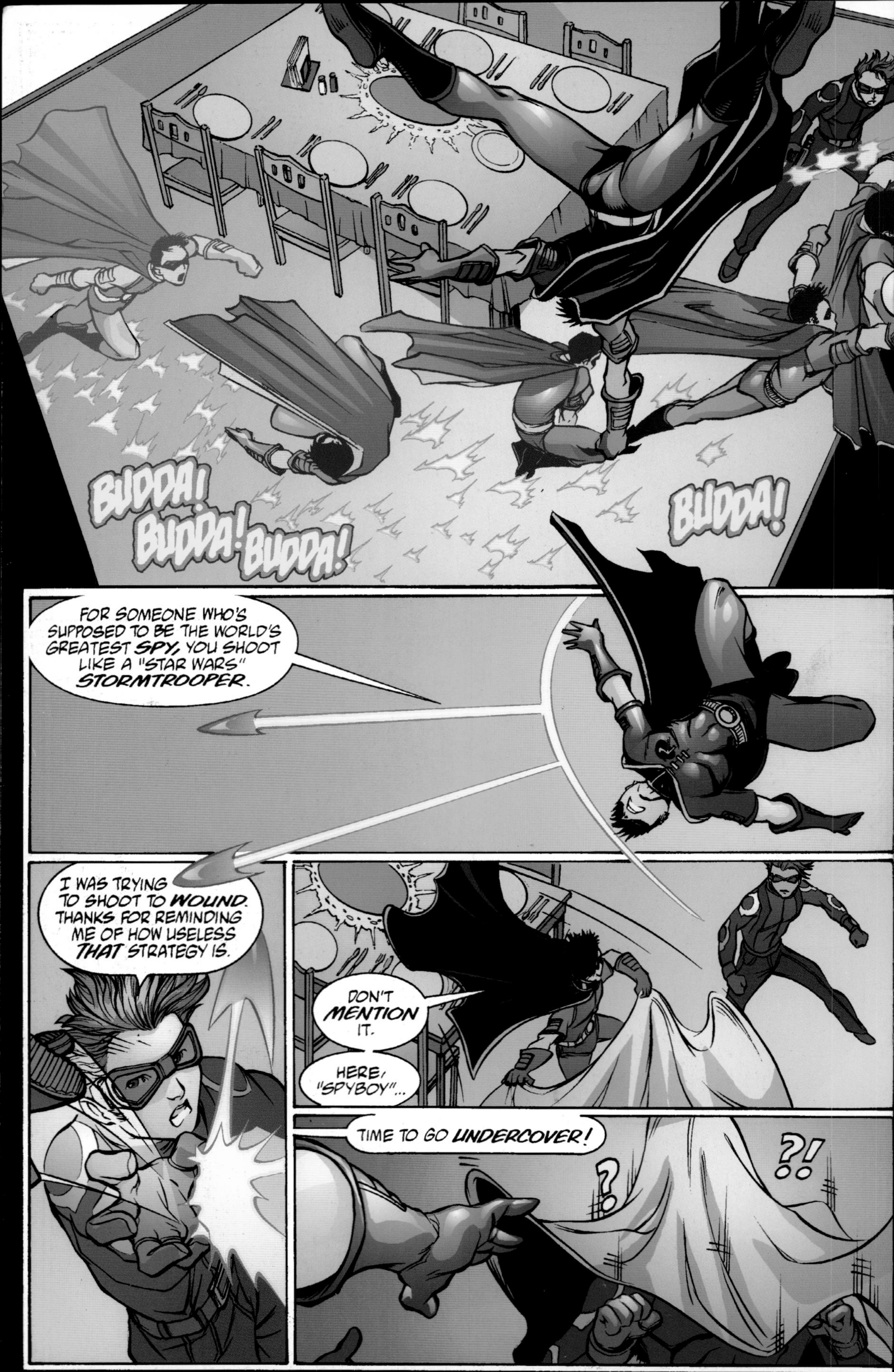
BUDDA! BUDDA! BUDDA!
BUDDA!
FOR SOMEONE WHO'S SUPPOSED TO BE THE WORLD'S GREATEST SPY, YOU SHOOT LIKE A "STAR WARS" STORMTROOPER.
I WAS TRYING TO SHOOT TO WOUND. THANKS FOR REMINDING ME OF HOW USELESS THAT STRATEGY IS.
DON'T MENTION IT.
HERE, "SPYBOY"...
TIME TO GO UNDERCOVER!
?
?!

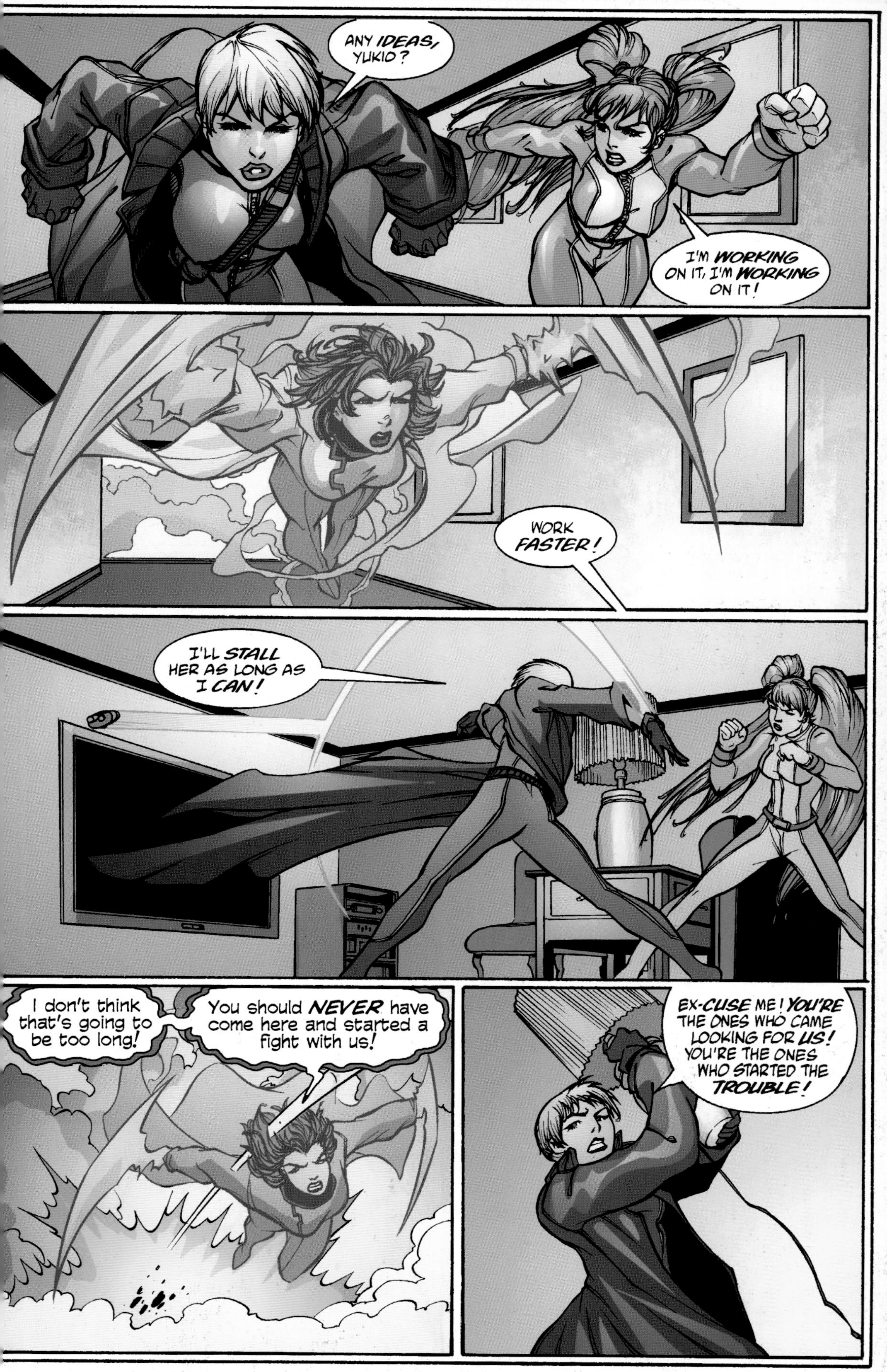
ANY IDEAS, YUKIO?
I'M WORKING ON IT, I'M WORKING ON IT!
WORK FASTER!
I'LL STALL HER AS LONG AS I CAN!
I don't think that's going to be too long!
You should NEVER have come here and started a fight with us!
EX-CUSE ME! YOU'RE THE ONES WHO CAME LOOKING FOR US! YOU'RE THE ONES WHO STARTED THE TROUBLE!

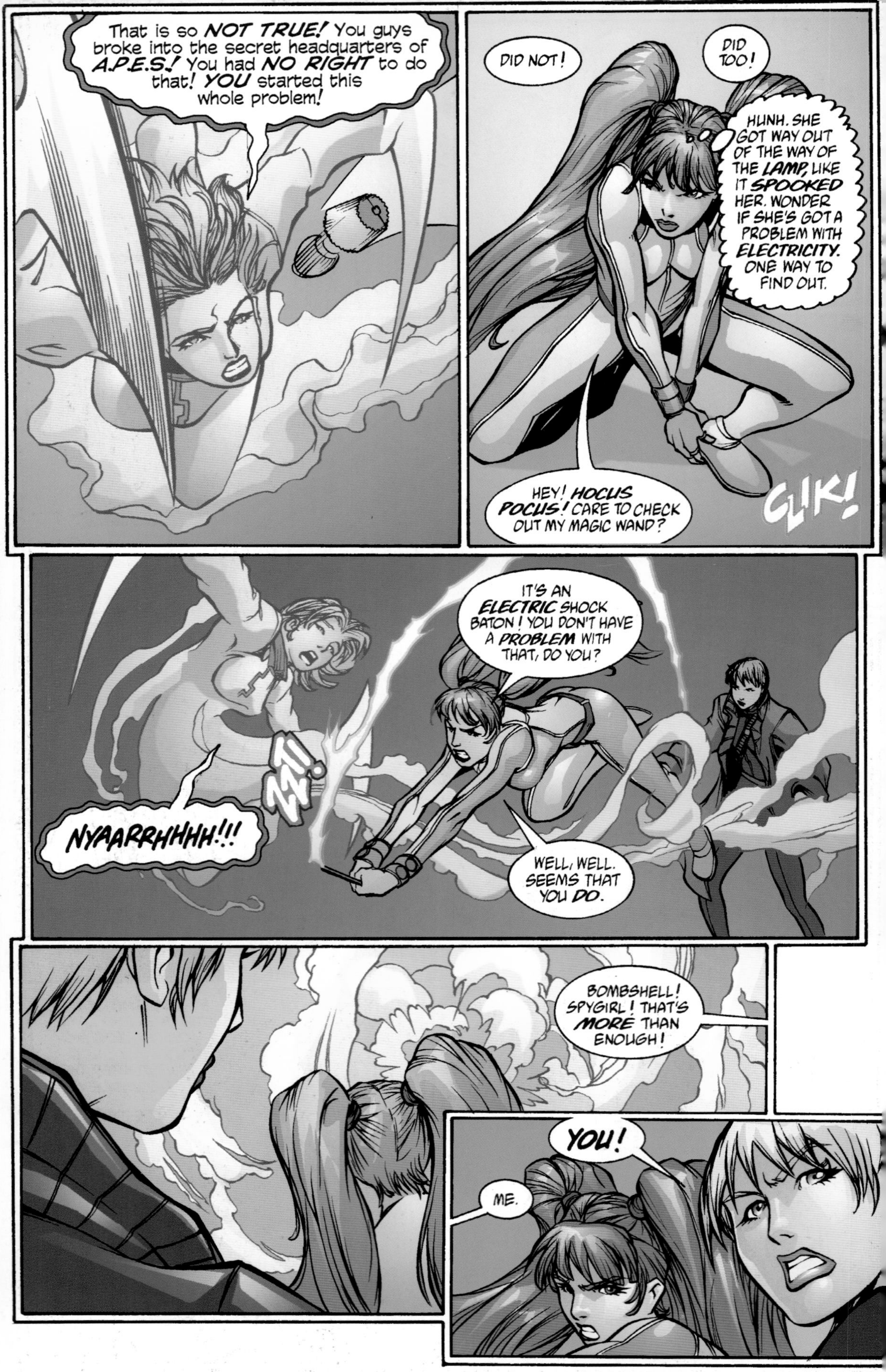
That is so NOT TRUE! You guys broke into the secret headquarters of A.P.E.S.! You had NO RIGHT to do that! YOU started this whole problem!
DID NOT!
DID TOO!
HUNH. SHE GOT WAY OUT OF THE WAY OF THE LAMP, LIKE IT SPOOKED HER. WONDER IF SHE'S GOT A PROBLEM WITH ELECTRICITY. ONE WAY TO FIND OUT.
HEY! HOCUS POCUS! CARE TO CHECK OUT MY MAGIC WAND?
CLIK!
IT'S AN ELECTRIC SHOCK BATON! YOU DON'T HAVE A PROBLEM WITH THAT, DO YOU?
ZZT!
NYAARRHHHH!!!
WELL, WELL. SEEMS THAT YOU DO.
BOMBSHELL! SPYGIRL! THAT'S MORE THAN ENOUGH!
YOU!
ME.

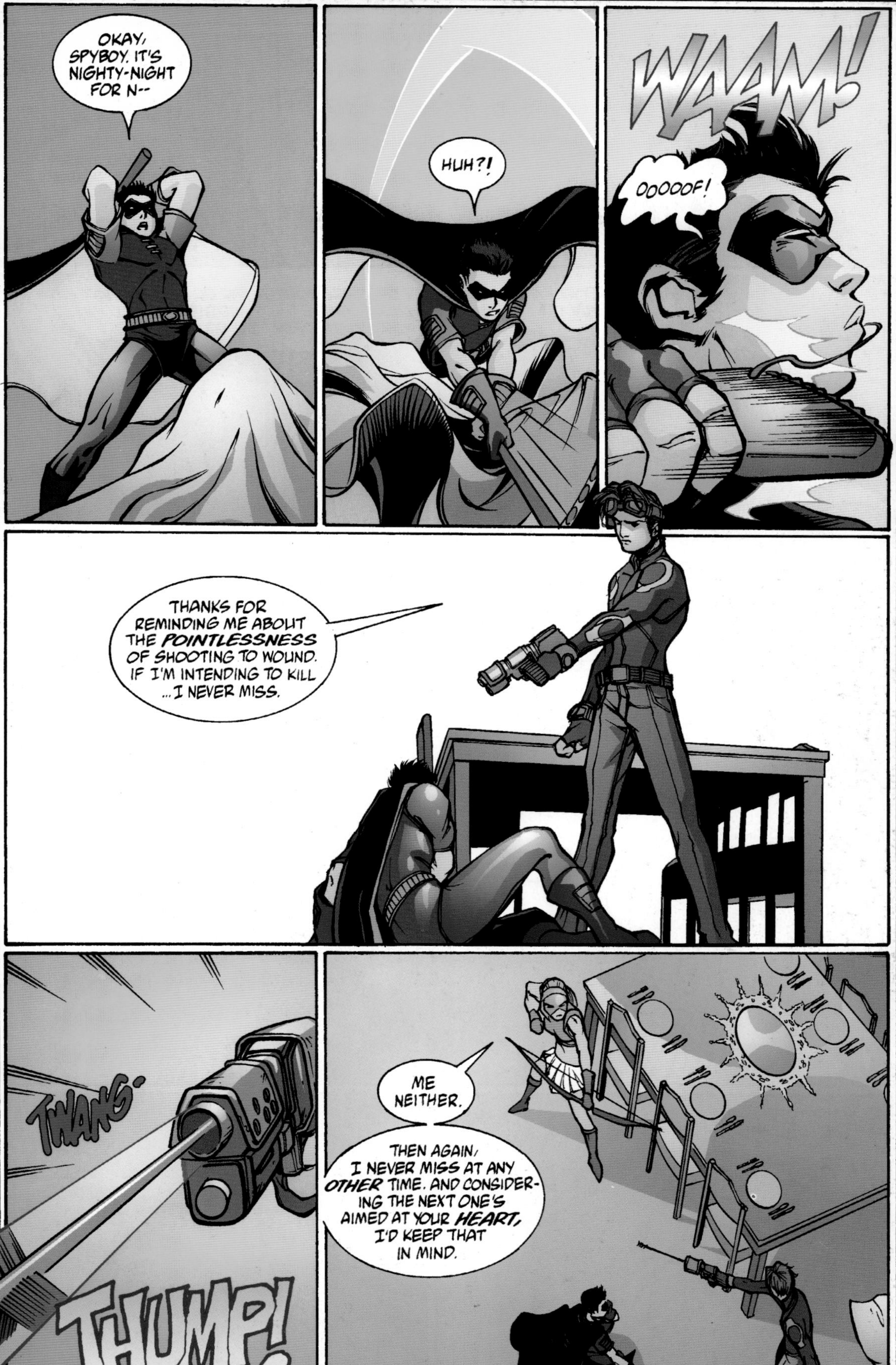
OKAY, SPYBOY. IT'S NIGHTY-NIGHT FOR N--
HUH?!
WAAM!
OOOOOF!
THANKS FOR REMINDING ME ABOUT THE *POINTLESSNESS* OF SHOOTING TO WOUND. IF I'M INTENDING TO KILL ...I NEVER MISS.
TWANG-
THUMP!
ME NEITHER.
THEN AGAIN, I NEVER MISS AT ANY *OTHER* TIME. AND CONSIDERING THE NEXT ONE'S AIMED AT YOUR *HEART,* I'D KEEP THAT IN MIND.

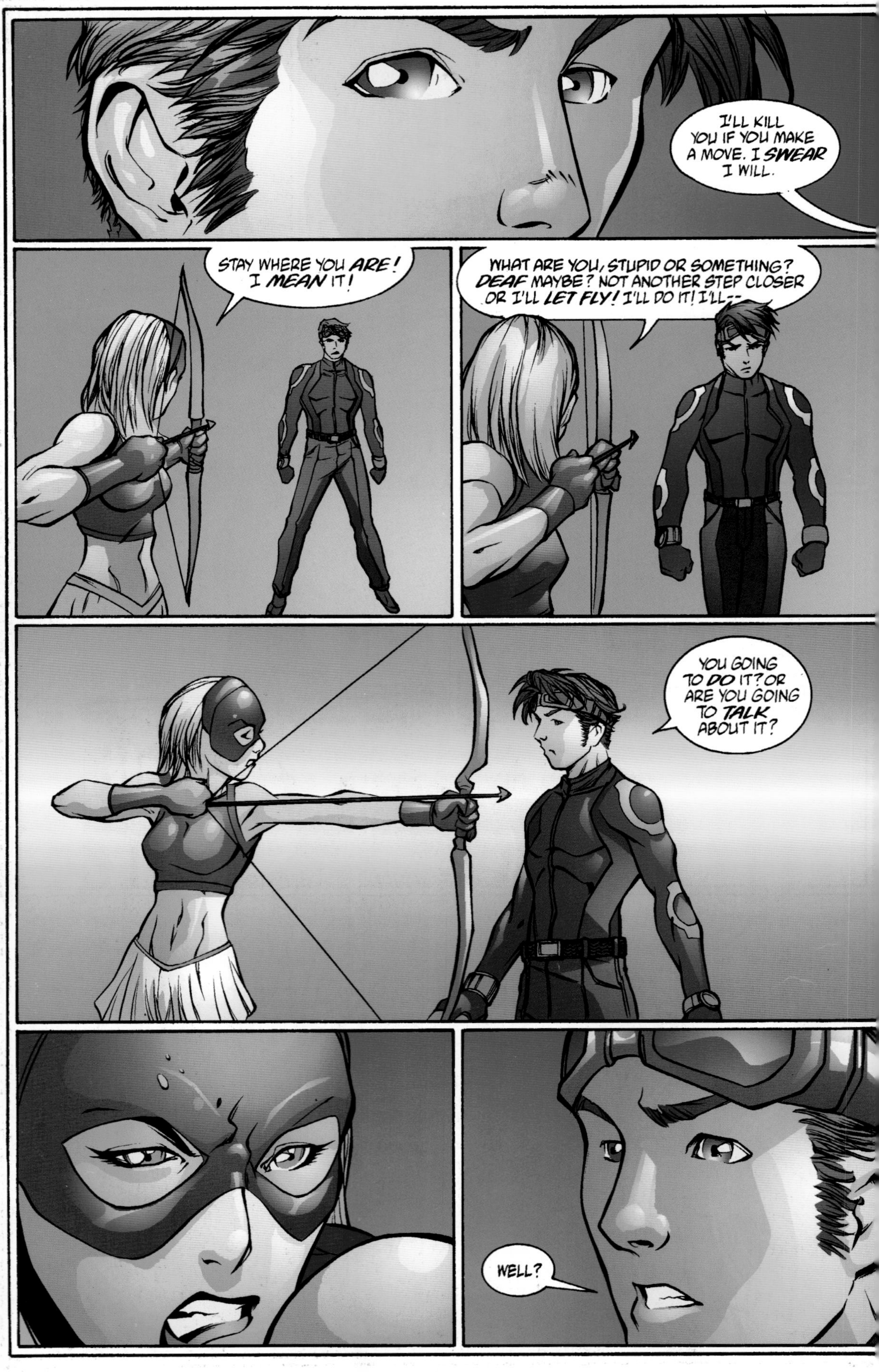
I'LL KILL YOU IF YOU MAKE A MOVE. I SWEAR I WILL.
STAY WHERE YOU ARE! I MEAN IT!
WHAT ARE YOU, STUPID OR SOMETHING? DEAF MAYBE? NOT ANOTHER STEP CLOSER OR I'LL LET FLY! I'LL DO IT! I'LL--
YOU GOING TO DO IT? OR ARE YOU GOING TO TALK ABOUT IT?
WELL?

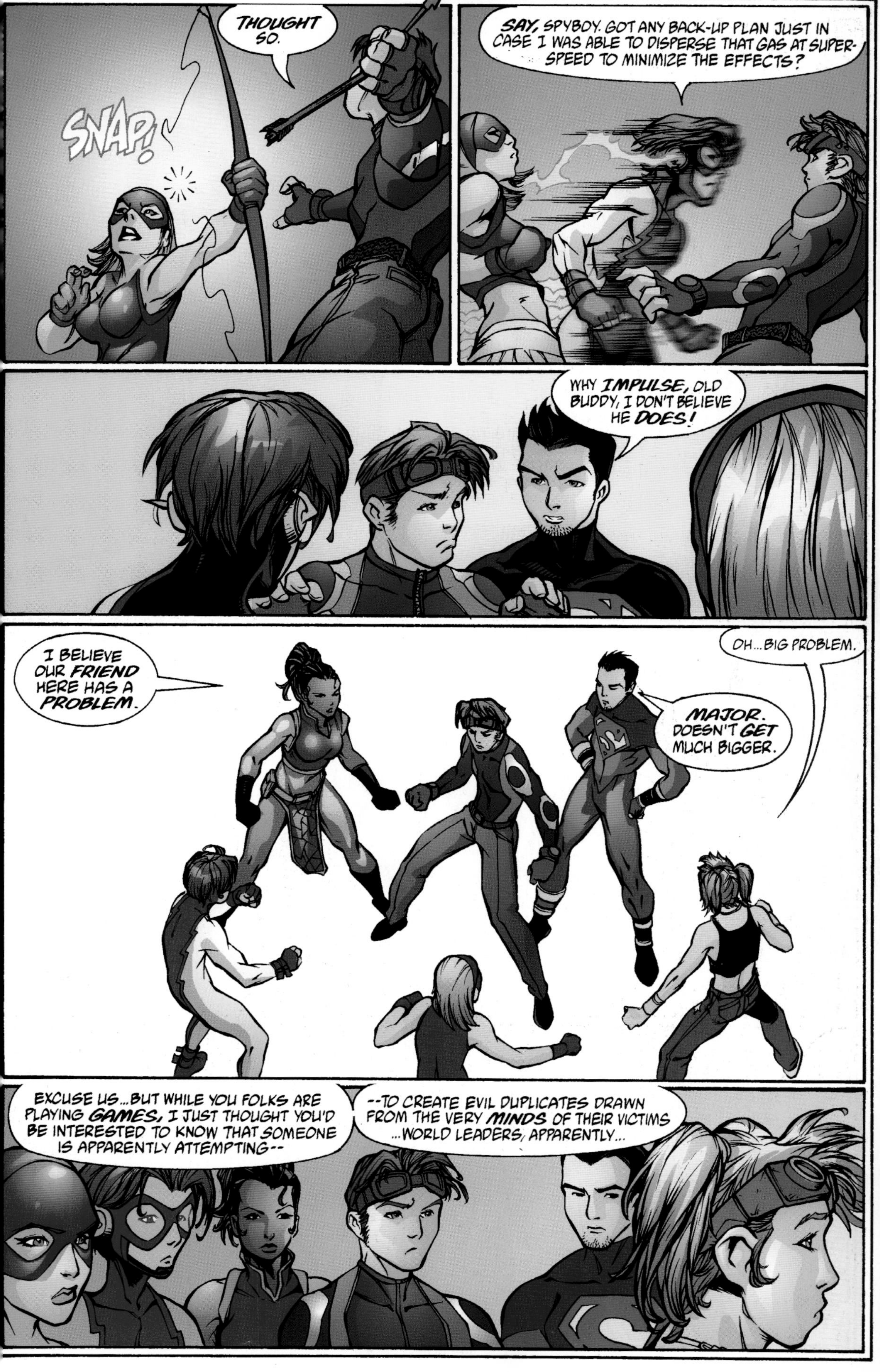
THOUGHT SO.
SNAP!
SAY, SPYBOY. GOT ANY BACK-UP PLAN JUST IN CASE I WAS ABLE TO DISPERSE THAT GAS AT SUPER-SPEED TO MINIMIZE THE EFFECTS?
WHY IMPULSE, OLD BUDDY, I DON'T BELIEVE HE DOES!
I BELIEVE OUR FRIEND HERE HAS A PROBLEM.
OH...BIG PROBLEM.
MAJOR. DOESN'T GET MUCH BIGGER.
EXCUSE US...BUT WHILE YOU FOLKS ARE PLAYING GAMES, I JUST THOUGHT YOU'D BE INTERESTED TO KNOW THAT SOMEONE IS APPARENTLY ATTEMPTING--
--TO CREATE EVIL DUPLICATES DRAWN FROM THE VERY MINDS OF THEIR VICTIMS ...WORLD LEADERS, APPARENTLY...

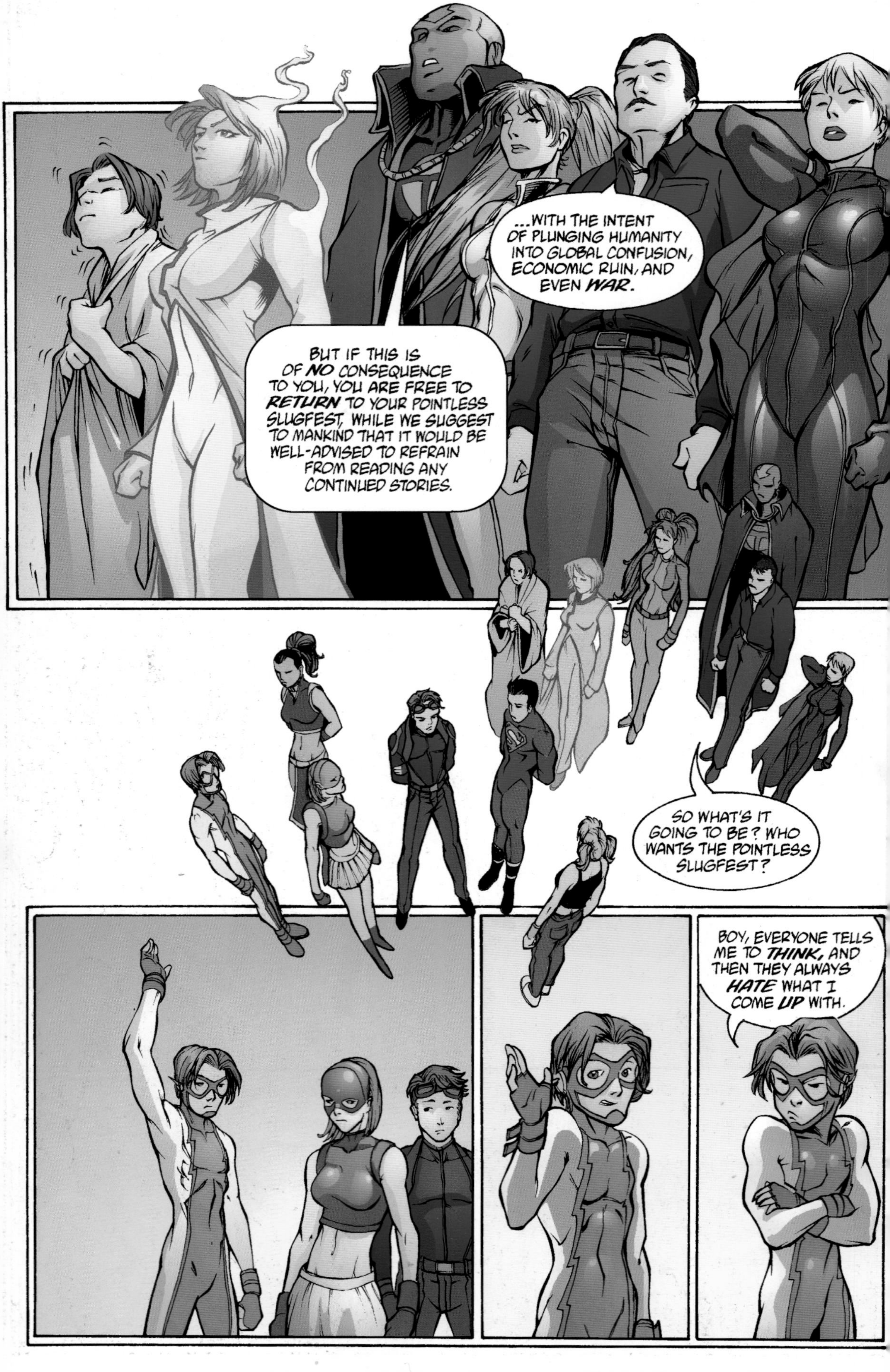
...WITH THE INTENT OF PLUNGING HUMANITY INTO GLOBAL CONFUSION, ECONOMIC RUIN, AND EVEN WAR.
BUT IF THIS IS OF NO CONSEQUENCE TO YOU, YOU ARE FREE TO RETURN TO YOUR POINTLESS SLUGFEST, WHILE WE SUGGEST TO MANKIND THAT IT WOULD BE WELL-ADVISED TO REFRAIN FROM READING ANY CONTINUED STORIES.
SO WHAT'S IT GOING TO BE? WHO WANTS THE POINTLESS SLUGFEST?
BOY, EVERYONE TELLS ME TO THINK, AND THEN THEY ALWAYS HATE WHAT I COME UP WITH.

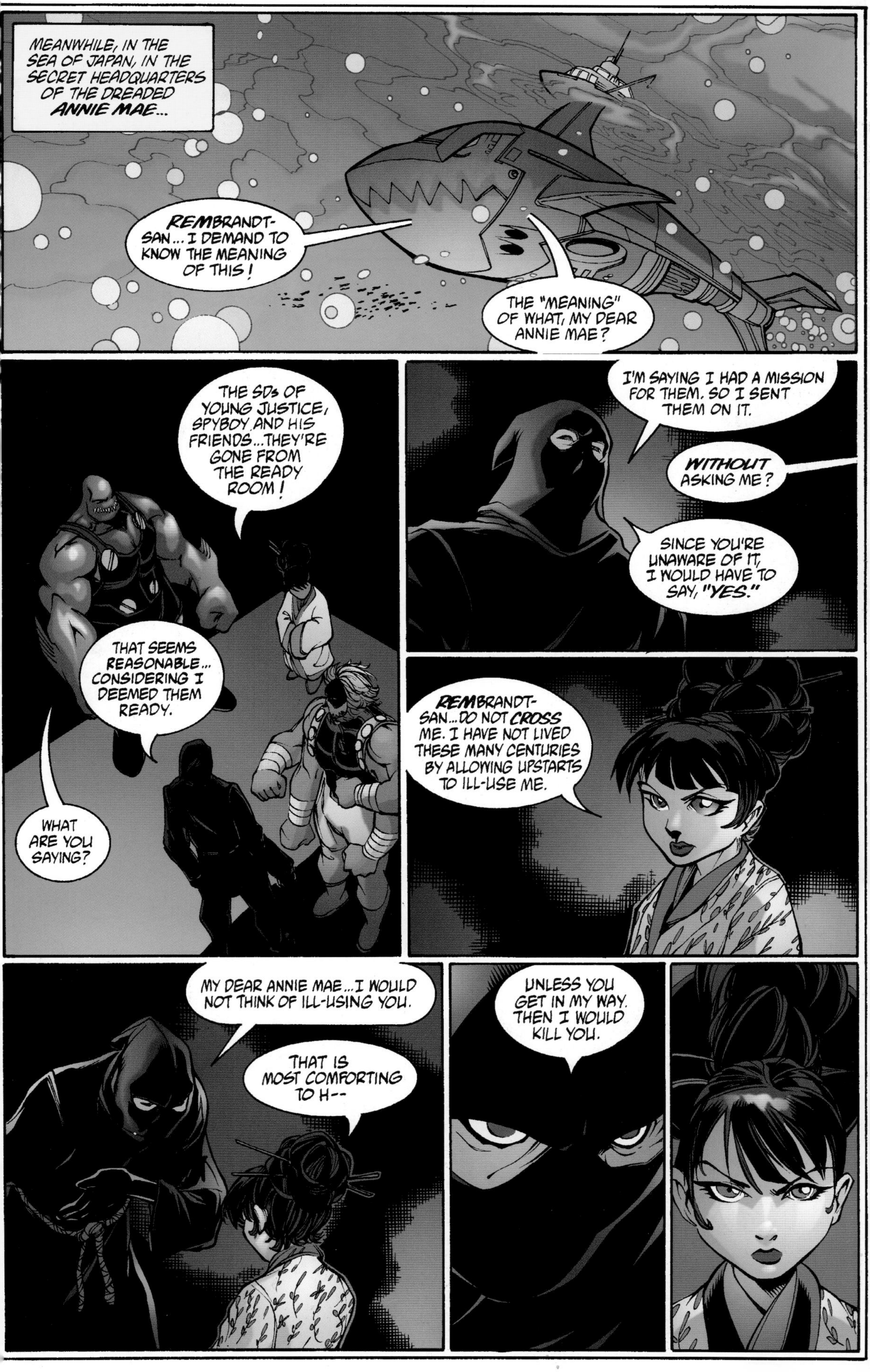
MEANWHILE, IN THE SEA OF JAPAN, IN THE SECRET HEADQUARTERS OF THE DREADED ANNIE MAE...
REMBRANDT-SAN... I DEMAND TO KNOW THE MEANING OF THIS!
THE "MEANING" OF WHAT, MY DEAR ANNIE MAE?
THE SDs OF YOUNG JUSTICE, SPYBOY AND HIS FRIENDS... THEY'RE GONE FROM THE READY ROOM!
THAT SEEMS REASONABLE... CONSIDERING I DEEMED THEM READY.
WHAT ARE YOU SAYING?
I'M SAYING I HAD A MISSION FOR THEM. SO I SENT THEM ON IT.
WITHOUT ASKING ME?
SINCE YOU'RE UNAWARE OF IT, I WOULD HAVE TO SAY, "YES."
REMBRANDT-SAN... DO NOT CROSS ME. I HAVE NOT LIVED THESE MANY CENTURIES BY ALLOWING UPSTARTS TO ILL-USE ME.
MY DEAR ANNIE MAE... I WOULD NOT THINK OF ILL-USING YOU.
THAT IS MOST COMFORTING TO H--
UNLESS YOU GET IN MY WAY. THEN I WOULD KILL YOU.

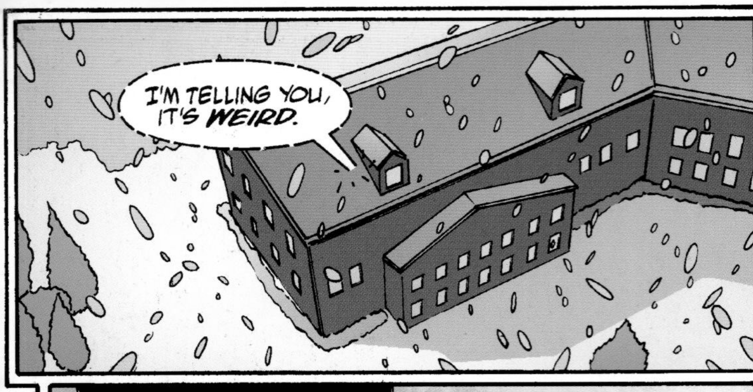
I'M TELLING YOU, IT'S **WEIRD**.

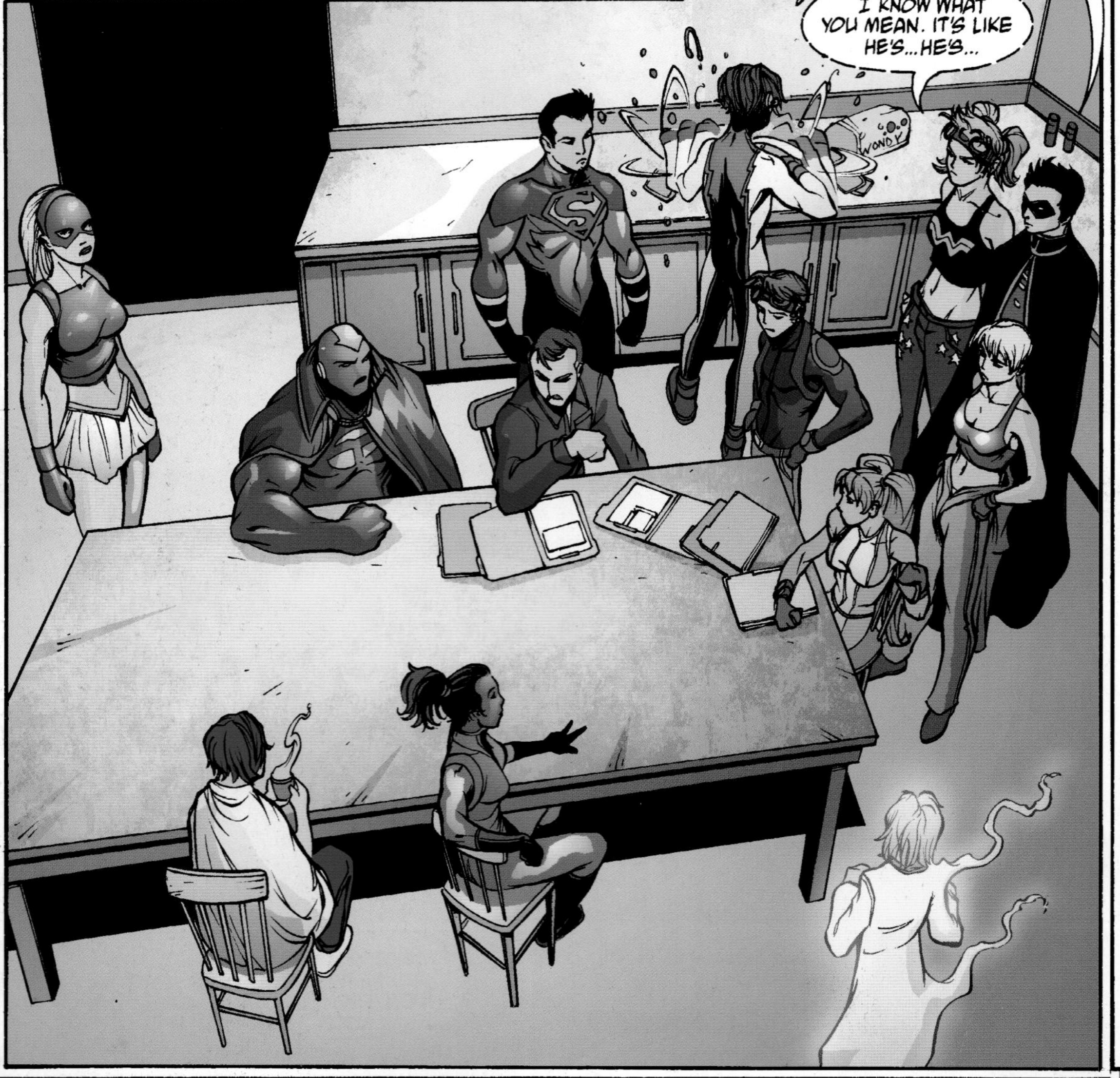
BATMAN NOTWITHSTANDING, USUALLY WHEN SOMEONE HAS A DOUBLE IDENTITY YOU CAN SEE **SOME** SIMILARITIES. POSTURE, TICS, REPEATED FIGURES OF SPEECH.
BUT ***SPYBOY*** AND ***ALEX FLEMING***...
I KNOW WHAT YOU MEAN. IT'S LIKE HE'S... HE'S...
WONDY

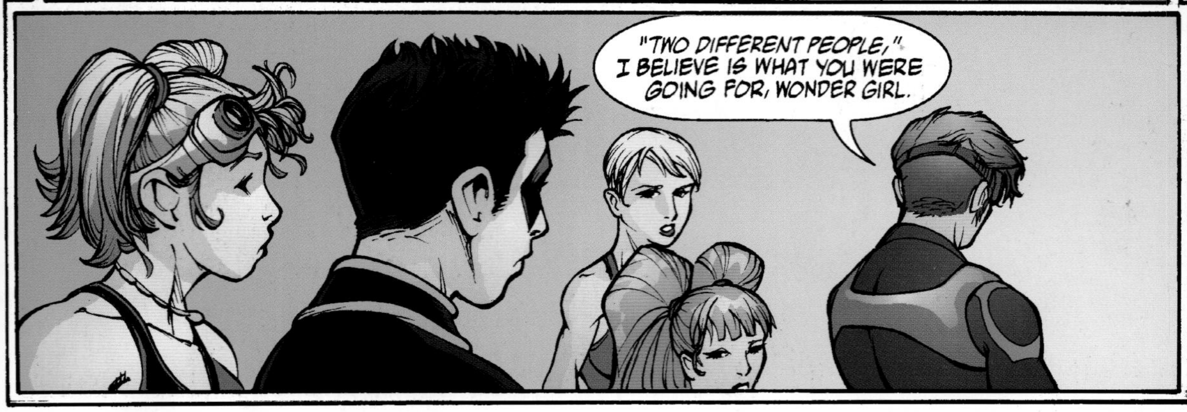
"TWO DIFFERENT PEOPLE," I BELIEVE IS WHAT YOU WERE GOING FOR, WONDER GIRL.

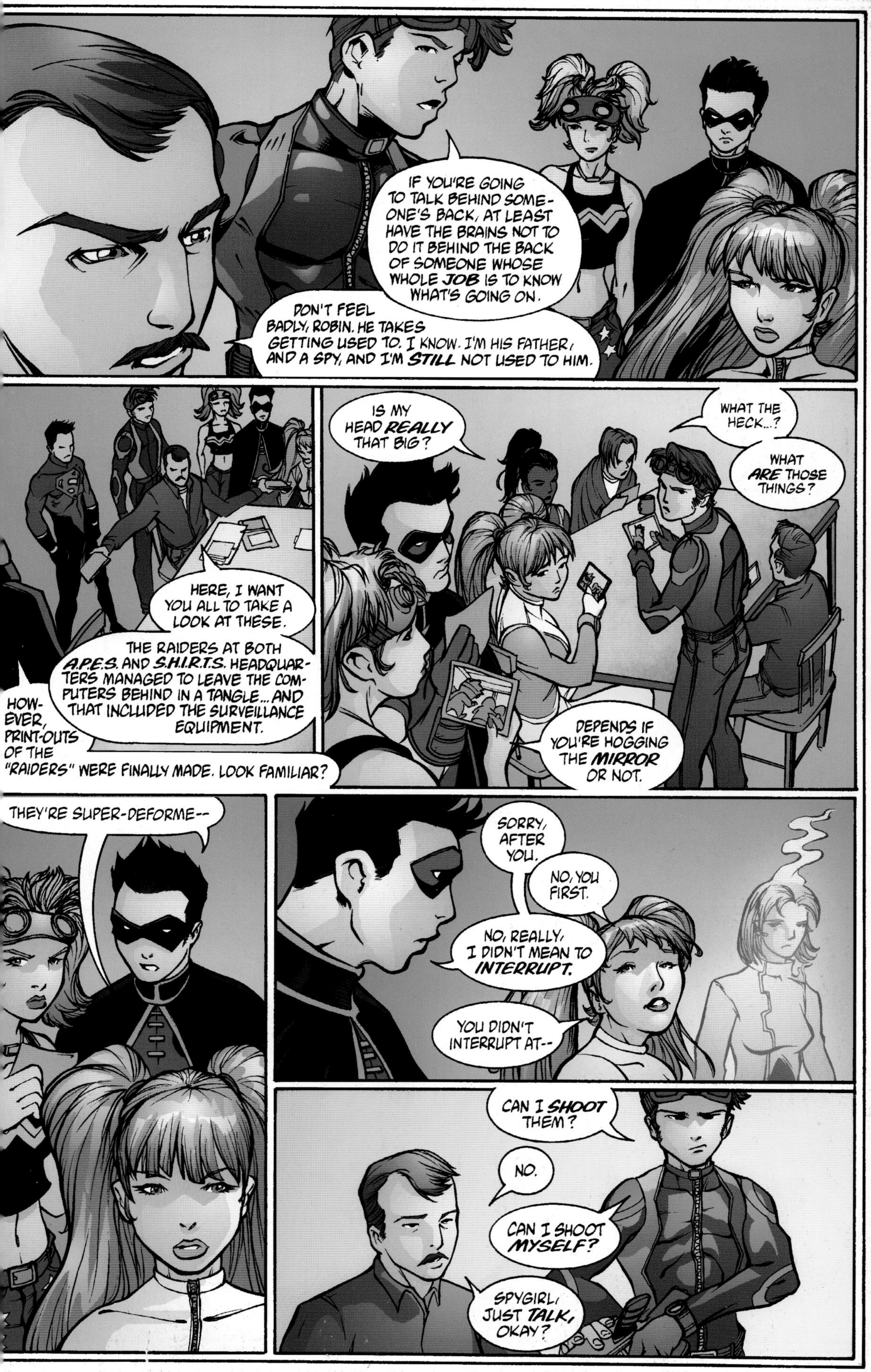
IF YOU'RE GOING TO TALK BEHIND SOME-ONE'S BACK, AT LEAST HAVE THE BRAINS NOT TO DO IT BEHIND THE BACK OF SOMEONE WHOSE WHOLE **JOB** IS TO KNOW WHAT'S GOING ON.
DON'T FEEL BADLY, ROBIN. HE TAKES GETTING USED TO. I KNOW. I'M HIS FATHER, AND A SPY, AND I'M ***STILL*** NOT USED TO HIM.
HERE, I WANT YOU ALL TO TAKE A LOOK AT THESE.
THE RAIDERS AT BOTH ***A.P.E.S.*** AND ***S.H.I.R.T.S.*** HEADQUAR-TERS MANAGED TO LEAVE THE COM-PUTERS BEHIND IN A TANGLE... AND THAT INCLUDED THE SURVEILLANCE EQUIPMENT.
HOW-EVER, PRINT-OUTS OF THE "RAIDERS" WERE FINALLY MADE. LOOK FAMILIAR?
IS MY HEAD ***REALLY*** THAT BIG?
WHAT THE HECK...?
WHAT ***ARE*** THOSE THINGS?
DEPENDS IF YOU'RE HOGGING THE ***MIRROR*** OR NOT.
THEY'RE SUPER-DEFORME--
SORRY, AFTER YOU.
NO, YOU FIRST.
NO, REALLY, I DIDN'T MEAN TO ***INTERRUPT.***
YOU DIDN'T INTERRUPT AT--
CAN I ***SHOOT*** THEM?
NO.
CAN I SHOOT ***MYSELF?***
SPYGIRL, JUST ***TALK,*** OKAY?

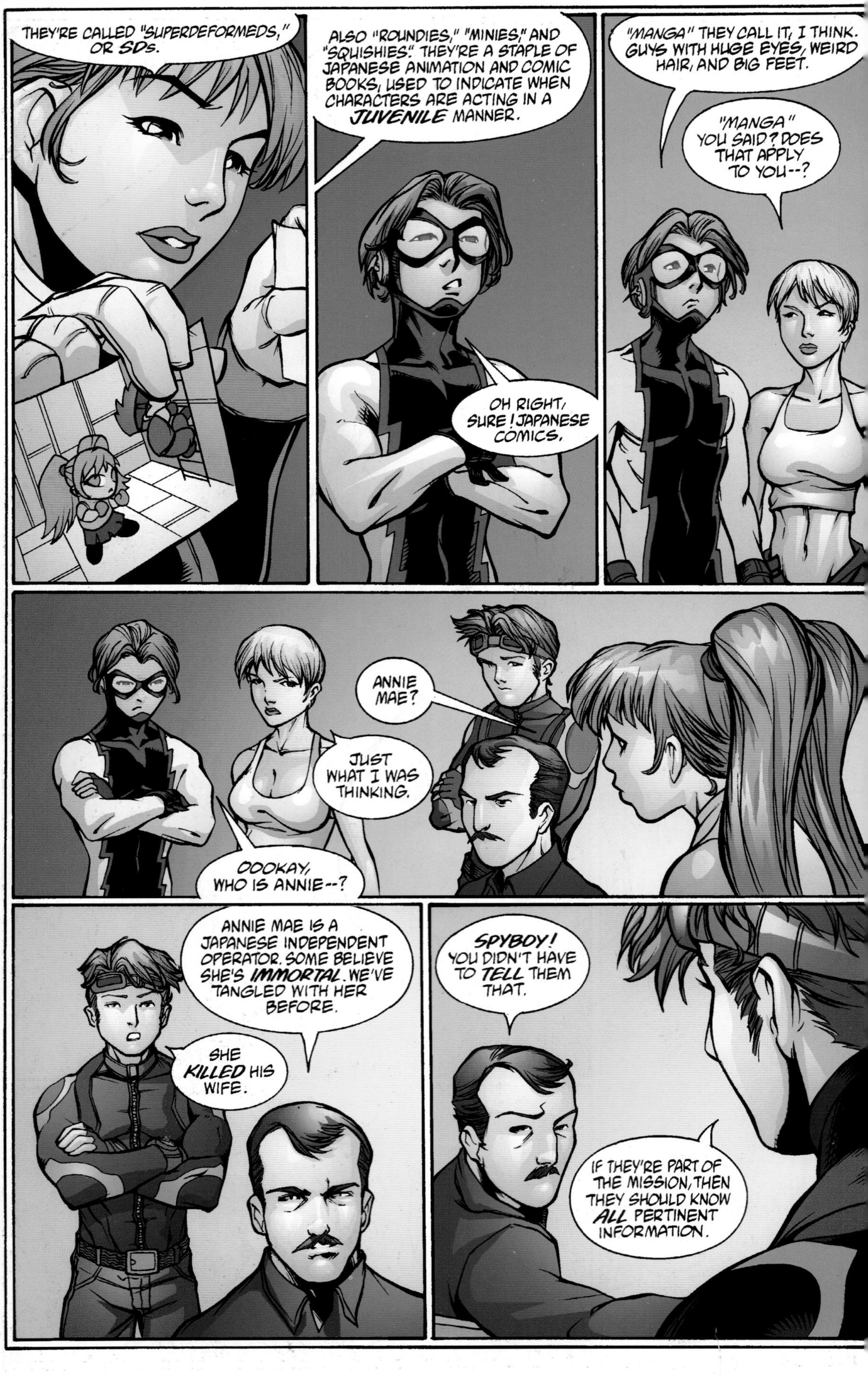
THEY'RE CALLED "SUPERDEFORMEDS," OR SDs.
ALSO "ROUNDIES," "MINIES," AND "SQUISHIES." THEY'RE A STAPLE OF JAPANESE ANIMATION AND COMIC BOOKS, USED TO INDICATE WHEN CHARACTERS ARE ACTING IN A JUVENILE MANNER.
OH RIGHT, SURE! JAPANESE COMICS.
"MANGA" THEY CALL IT, I THINK. GUYS WITH HUGE EYES, WEIRD HAIR, AND BIG FEET.
"MANGA" YOU SAID? DOES THAT APPLY TO YOU--?
JUST WHAT I WAS THINKING.
OOOKAY, WHO IS ANNIE--?
ANNIE MAE?
ANNIE MAE IS A JAPANESE INDEPENDENT OPERATOR. SOME BELIEVE SHE'S IMMORTAL. WE'VE TANGLED WITH HER BEFORE.
SHE KILLED HIS WIFE.
SPYBOY! YOU DIDN'T HAVE TO TELL THEM THAT.
IF THEY'RE PART OF THE MISSION, THEN THEY SHOULD KNOW ALL PERTINENT INFORMATION.

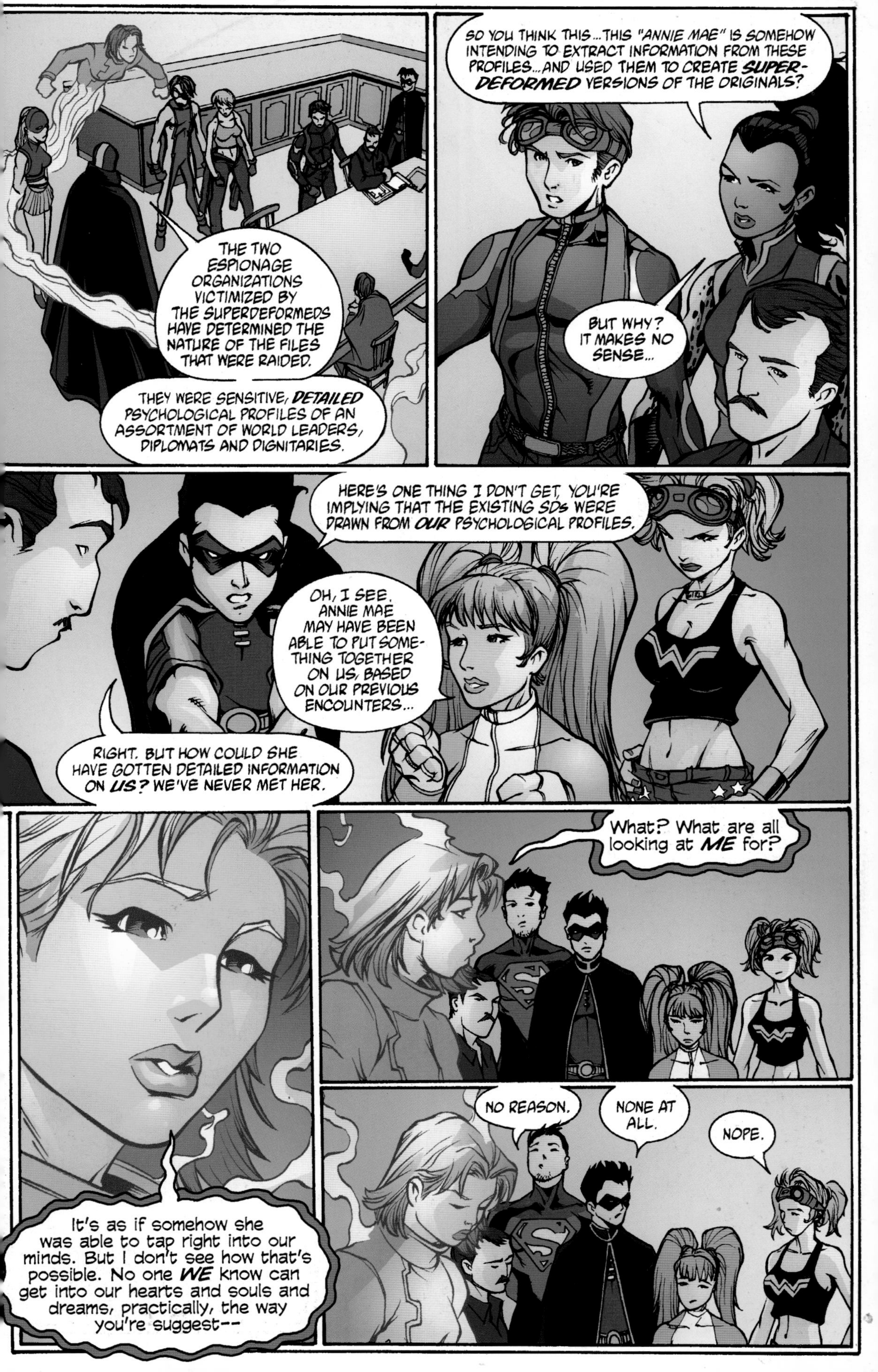
THE TWO ESPIONAGE ORGANIZATIONS VICTIMIZED BY THE SUPERDEFORMEDS HAVE DETERMINED THE NATURE OF THE FILES THAT WERE RAIDED.
THEY WERE SENSITIVE, DETAILED PSYCHOLOGICAL PROFILES OF AN ASSORTMENT OF WORLD LEADERS, DIPLOMATS AND DIGNITARIES.
SO YOU THINK THIS... THIS "ANNIE MAE" IS SOMEHOW INTENDING TO EXTRACT INFORMATION FROM THESE PROFILES... AND USED THEM TO CREATE SUPER-DEFORMED VERSIONS OF THE ORIGINALS?
BUT WHY? IT MAKES NO SENSE...
HERE'S ONE THING I DON'T GET, YOU'RE IMPLYING THAT THE EXISTING SDs WERE DRAWN FROM OUR PSYCHOLOGICAL PROFILES.
OH, I SEE. ANNIE MAE MAY HAVE BEEN ABLE TO PUT SOME-THING TOGETHER ON US, BASED ON OUR PREVIOUS ENCOUNTERS...
RIGHT. BUT HOW COULD SHE HAVE GOTTEN DETAILED INFORMATION ON US? WE'VE NEVER MET HER.
It's as if somehow she was able to tap right into our minds. But I don't see how that's possible. No one WE know can get into our hearts and souls and dreams, practically, the way you're suggest--
What? What are all looking at ME for?
NO REASON.
NONE AT ALL.
NOPE.

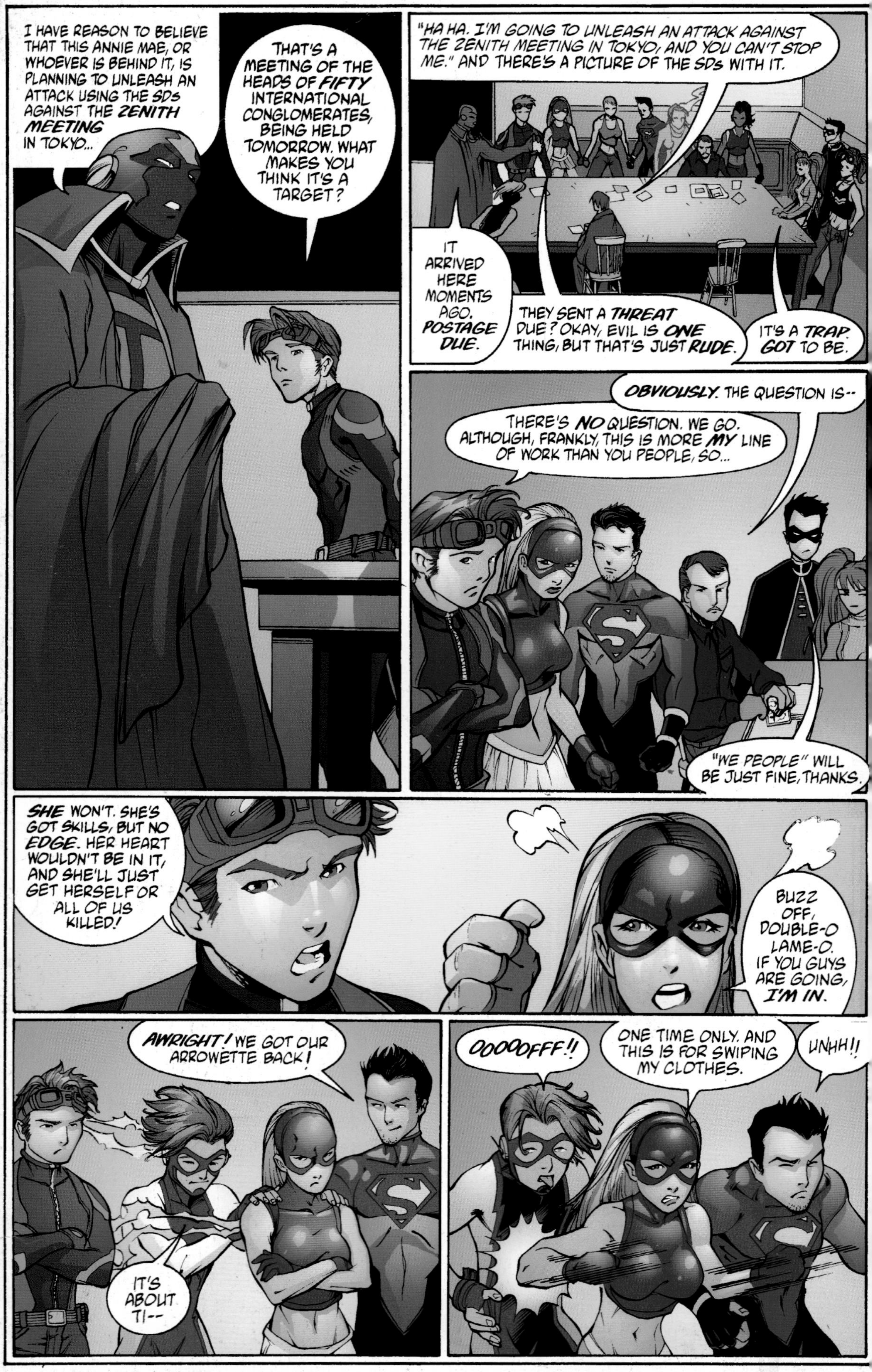
I HAVE REASON TO BELIEVE THAT THIS ANNIE MAE, OR WHOEVER IS BEHIND IT, IS PLANNING TO UNLEASH AN ATTACK USING THE SDs AGAINST THE ZENITH MEETING IN TOKYO...
THAT'S A MEETING OF THE HEADS OF FIFTY INTERNATIONAL CONGLOMERATES, BEING HELD TOMORROW. WHAT MAKES YOU THINK IT'S A TARGET?
"HA HA. I'M GOING TO UNLEASH AN ATTACK AGAINST THE ZENITH MEETING IN TOKYO, AND YOU CAN'T STOP ME." AND THERE'S A PICTURE OF THE SDs WITH IT.
IT ARRIVED HERE MOMENTS AGO. POSTAGE DUE.
THEY SENT A THREAT DUE? OKAY, EVIL IS ONE THING, BUT THAT'S JUST RUDE.
IT'S A TRAP. GOT TO BE.
OBVIOUSLY. THE QUESTION IS--
THERE'S NO QUESTION. WE GO. ALTHOUGH, FRANKLY, THIS IS MORE MY LINE OF WORK THAN YOU PEOPLE, SO...
"WE PEOPLE" WILL BE JUST FINE, THANKS.
SHE WON'T. SHE'S GOT SKILLS, BUT NO EDGE. HER HEART WOULDN'T BE IN IT, AND SHE'LL JUST GET HERSELF OR ALL OF US KILLED!
BUZZ OFF, DOUBLE-O LAME-O. IF YOU GUYS ARE GOING, I'M IN.
AWRIGHT! WE GOT OUR ARROWETTE BACK!
IT'S ABOUT TI--
OOOOOFFF!!
ONE TIME ONLY. AND THIS IS FOR SWIPING MY CLOTHES.
UNHH!!

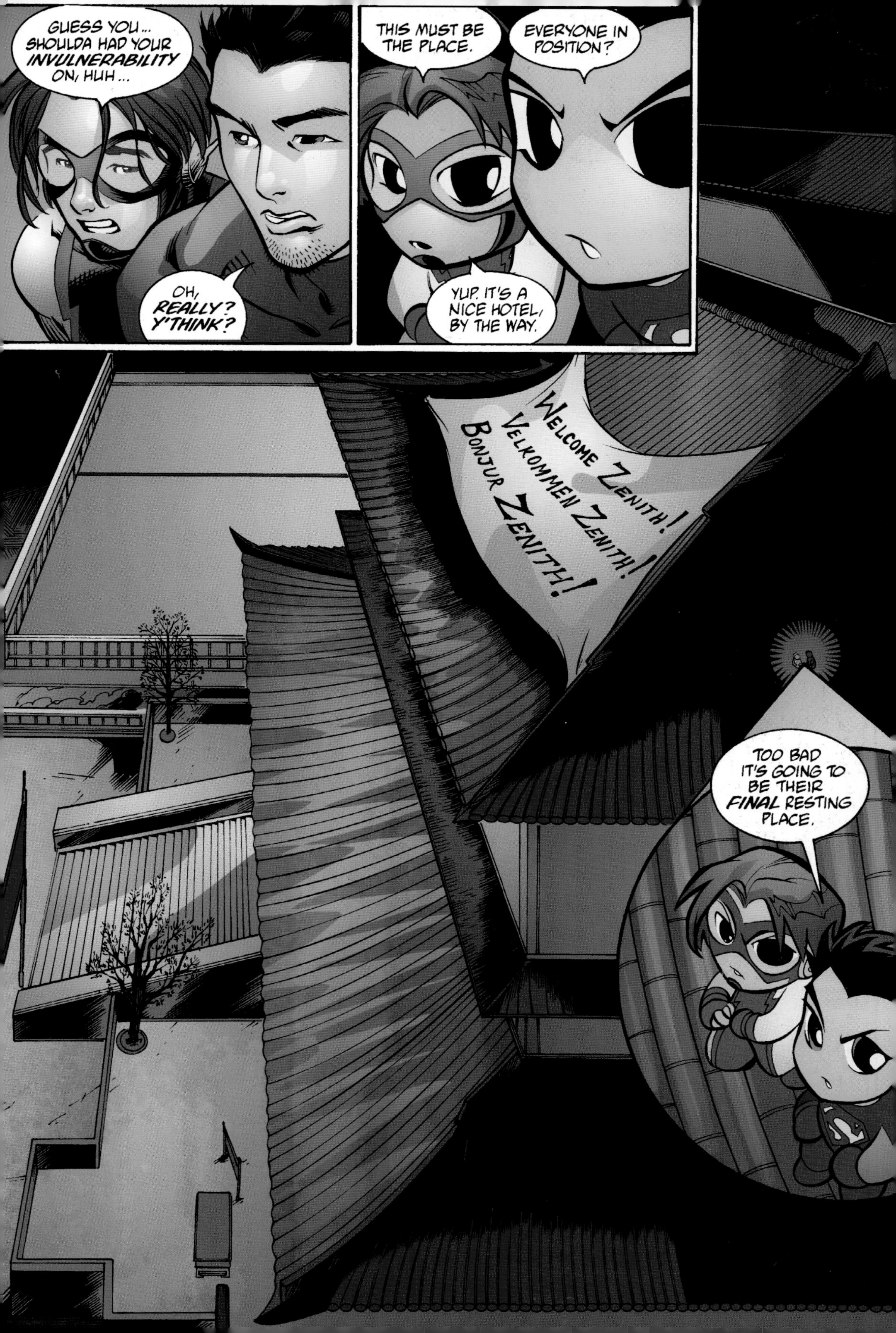
GUESS YOU... SHOULDA HAD YOUR *INVULNERABILITY* ON, HUH...
OH, *REALLY? Y'THINK?*
THIS MUST BE THE PLACE.
EVERYONE IN POSITION?
YUP. IT'S A NICE HOTEL, BY THE WAY.
WELCOME ZENITH!
VELKOMMEN ZENITH!
BONJUR ZENITH!
TOO BAD IT'S GOING TO BE THEIR *FINAL* RESTING PLACE.

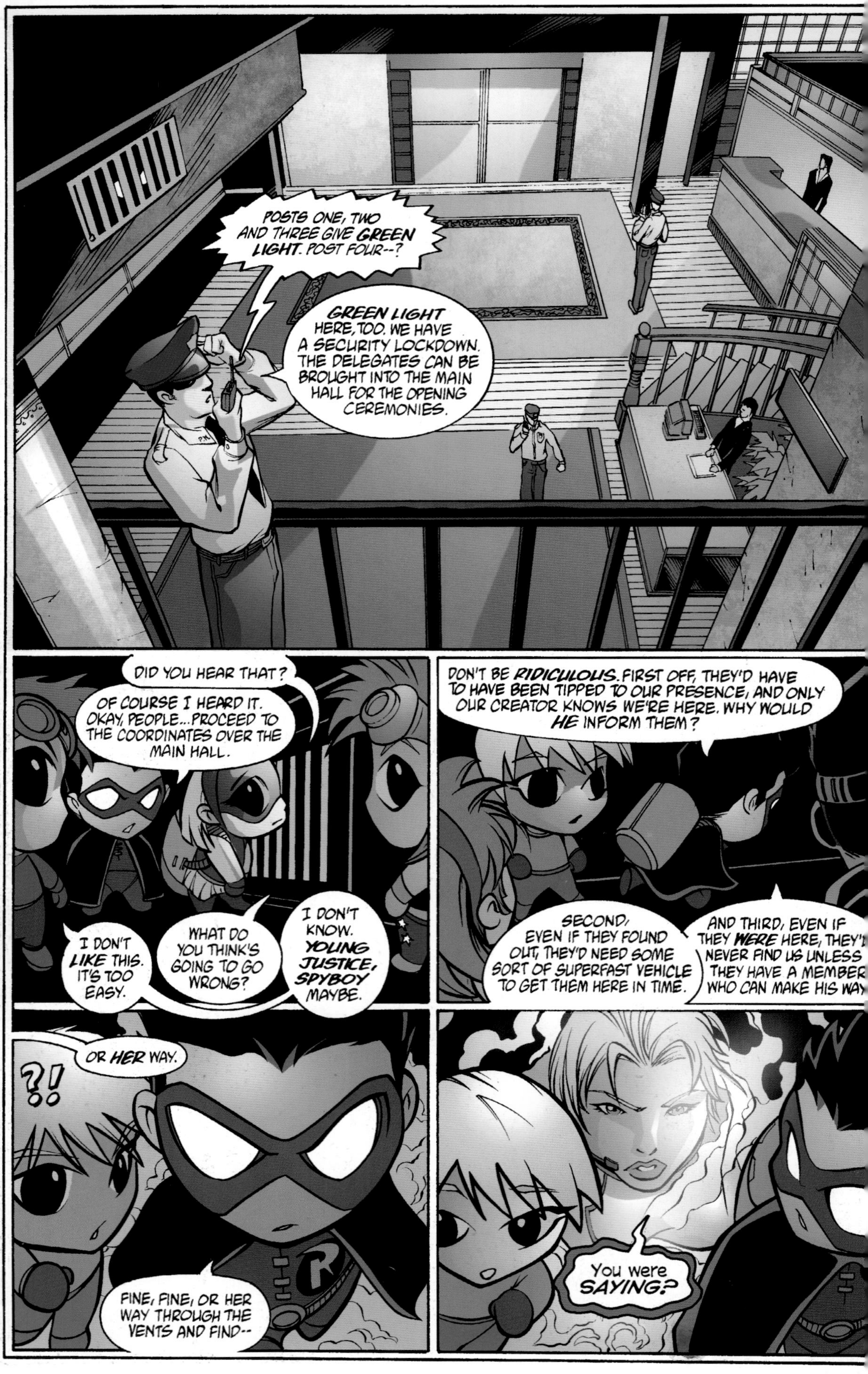

POSTS ONE, TWO AND THREE GIVE GREEN LIGHT. POST FOUR--?
GREEN LIGHT HERE, TOO. WE HAVE A SECURITY LOCKDOWN. THE DELEGATES CAN BE BROUGHT INTO THE MAIN HALL FOR THE OPENING CEREMONIES.
DID YOU HEAR THAT?
OF COURSE I HEARD IT. OKAY, PEOPLE...PROCEED TO THE COORDINATES OVER THE MAIN HALL.
I DON'T LIKE THIS. IT'S TOO EASY.
WHAT DO YOU THINK'S GOING TO GO WRONG?
I DON'T KNOW. YOUNG JUSTICE, SPYBOY MAYBE.
DON'T BE RIDICULOUS. FIRST OFF, THEY'D HAVE TO HAVE BEEN TIPPED TO OUR PRESENCE, AND ONLY OUR CREATOR KNOWS WE'RE HERE. WHY WOULD HE INFORM THEM?
SECOND, EVEN IF THEY FOUND OUT, THEY'D NEED SOME SORT OF SUPERFAST VEHICLE TO GET THEM HERE IN TIME.
AND THIRD, EVEN IF THEY WERE HERE, THEY'LL NEVER FIND US UNLESS THEY HAVE A MEMBER WHO CAN MAKE HIS WAY
OR HER WAY.
?!
FINE, FINE, OR HER WAY THROUGH THE VENTS AND FIND--
You were SAYING?

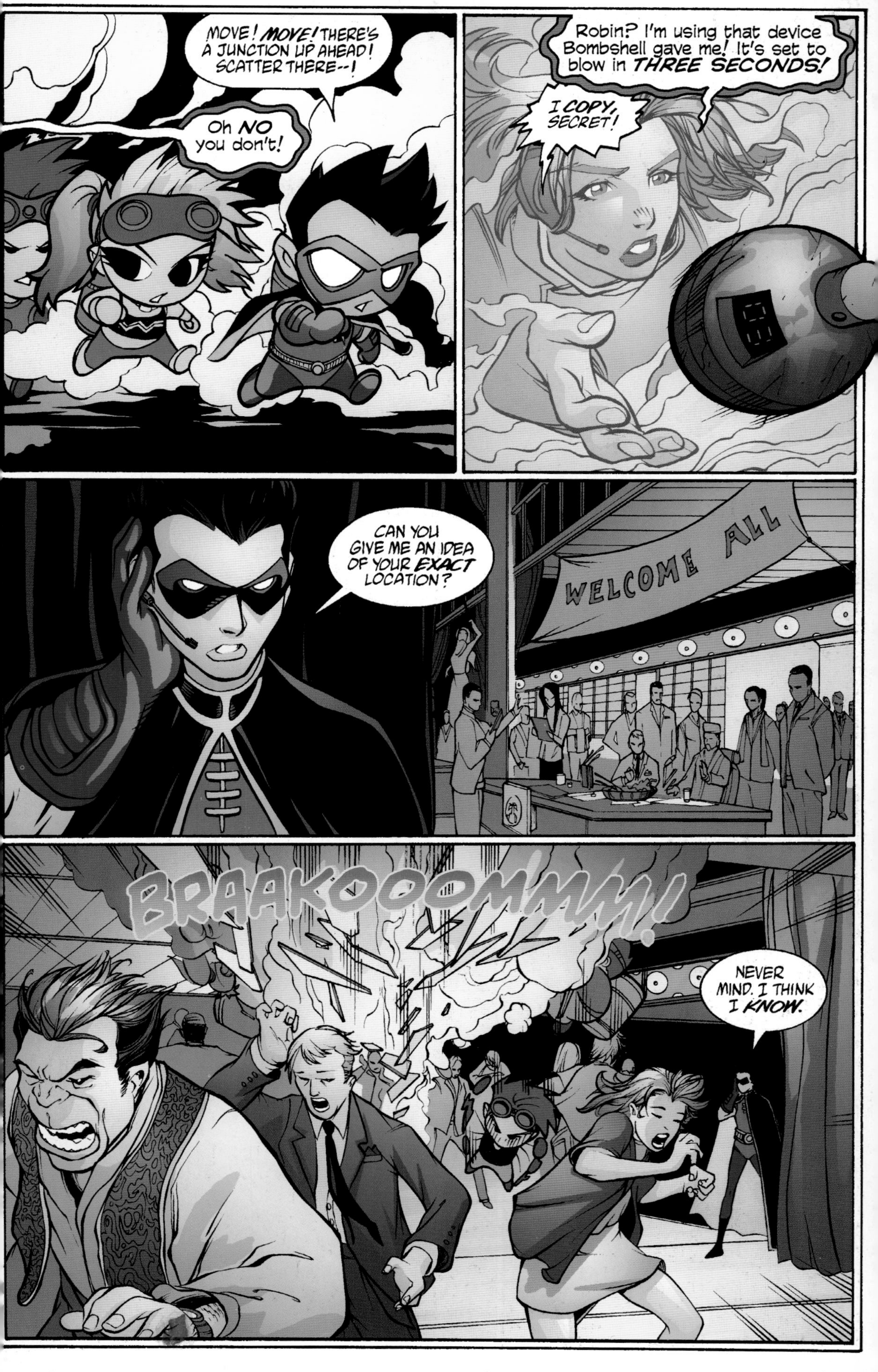
MOVE! MOVE! THERE'S A JUNCTION UP AHEAD! SCATTER THERE--!
Oh NO you don't!
Robin? I'm using that device Bombshell gave me! It's set to blow in THREE SECONDS!
I COPY, SECRET!
CAN YOU GIVE ME AN IDEA OF YOUR EXACT LOCATION?
WELCOME ALL
BRAAKOOOMMMM!
NEVER MIND. I THINK I KNOW.

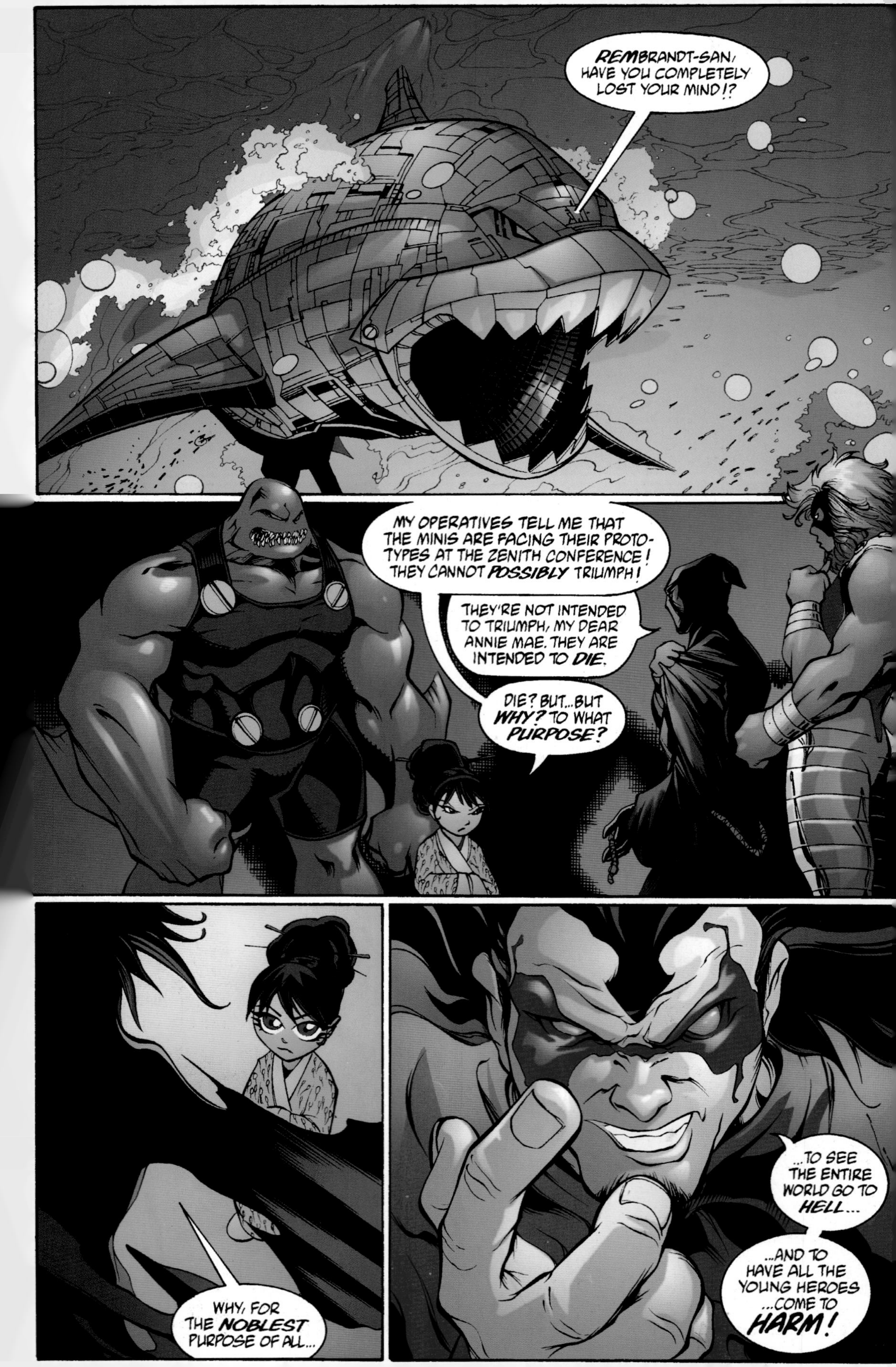
REMBRANDT-SAN, HAVE YOU COMPLETELY LOST YOUR MIND!?
MY OPERATIVES TELL ME THAT THE MINIS ARE FACING THEIR PROTOTYPES AT THE ZENITH CONFERENCE! THEY CANNOT POSSIBLY TRIUMPH!
THEY'RE NOT INTENDED TO TRIUMPH, MY DEAR ANNIE MAE. THEY ARE INTENDED TO DIE.
DIE? BUT...BUT WHY? TO WHAT PURPOSE?
WHY, FOR THE NOBLEST PURPOSE OF ALL...
...TO SEE THE ENTIRE WORLD GO TO HELL...
...AND TO HAVE ALL THE YOUNG HEROES ...COME TO HARM!

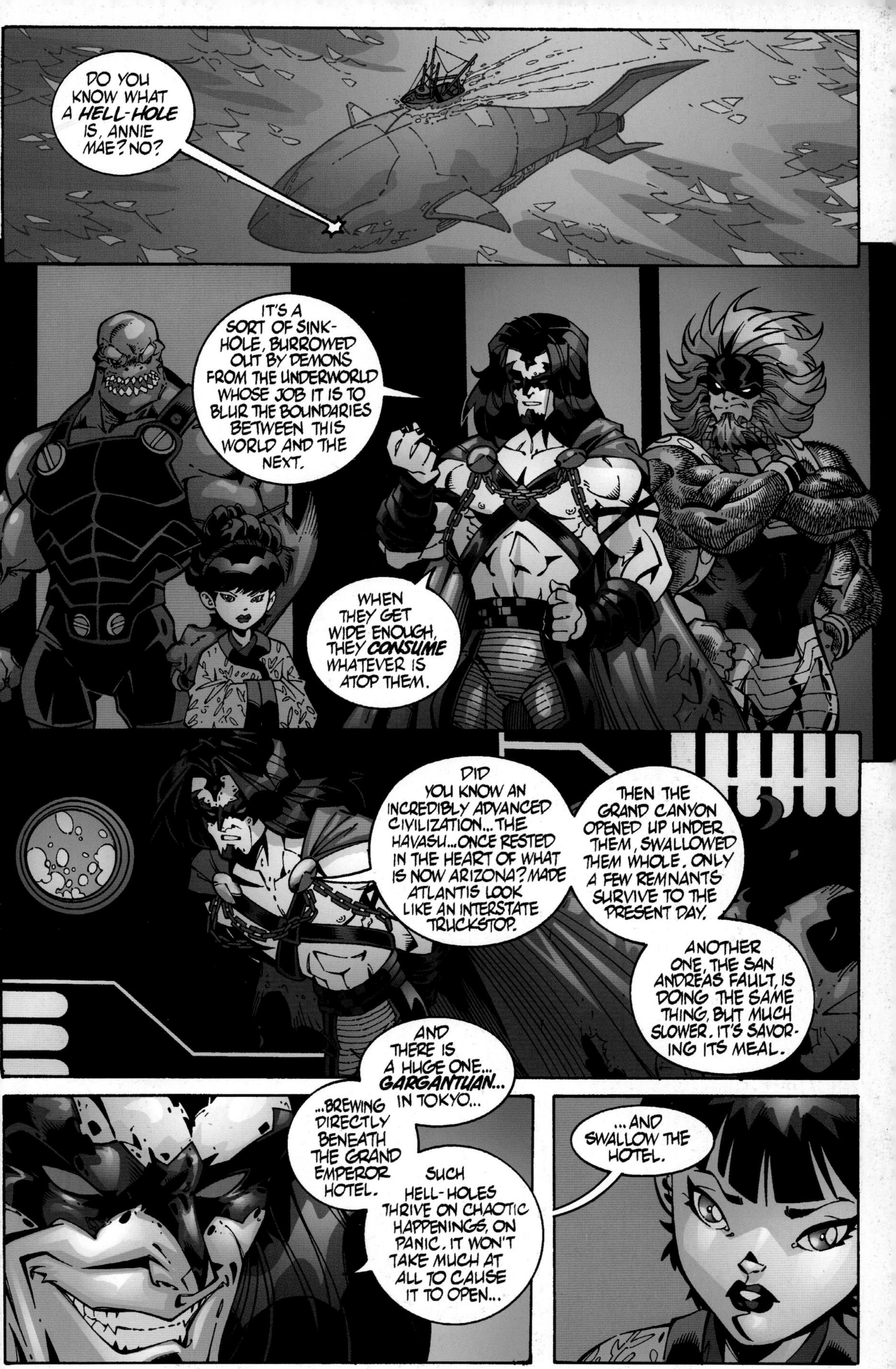
DO YOU KNOW WHAT A **HELL-HOLE** IS, ANNIE MAE? NO?
IT'S A SORT OF SINK-HOLE, BURROWED OUT BY DEMONS FROM THE UNDERWORLD WHOSE JOB IT IS TO BLUR THE BOUNDARIES BETWEEN THIS WORLD AND THE NEXT.
WHEN THEY GET WIDE ENOUGH, THEY **CONSUME** WHATEVER IS ATOP THEM.
DID YOU KNOW AN INCREDIBLY ADVANCED CIVILIZATION... THE HAVASU...ONCE RESTED IN THE HEART OF WHAT IS NOW ARIZONA? MADE ATLANTIS LOOK LIKE AN INTERSTATE TRUCKSTOP.
THEN THE GRAND CANYON OPENED UP UNDER THEM, SWALLOWED THEM WHOLE. ONLY A FEW REMNANTS SURVIVE TO THE PRESENT DAY.
ANOTHER ONE, THE SAN ANDREAS FAULT, IS DOING THE SAME THING, BUT MUCH SLOWER. IT'S SAVORING ITS MEAL.
AND THERE IS A HUGE ONE... **GARGANTUAN**... IN TOKYO...
...BREWING DIRECTLY BENEATH THE GRAND EMPEROR HOTEL.
SUCH HELL-HOLES THRIVE ON CHAOTIC HAPPENINGS, ON PANIC. IT WON'T TAKE MUCH AT ALL TO CAUSE IT TO OPEN...
...AND SWALLOW THE HOTEL.

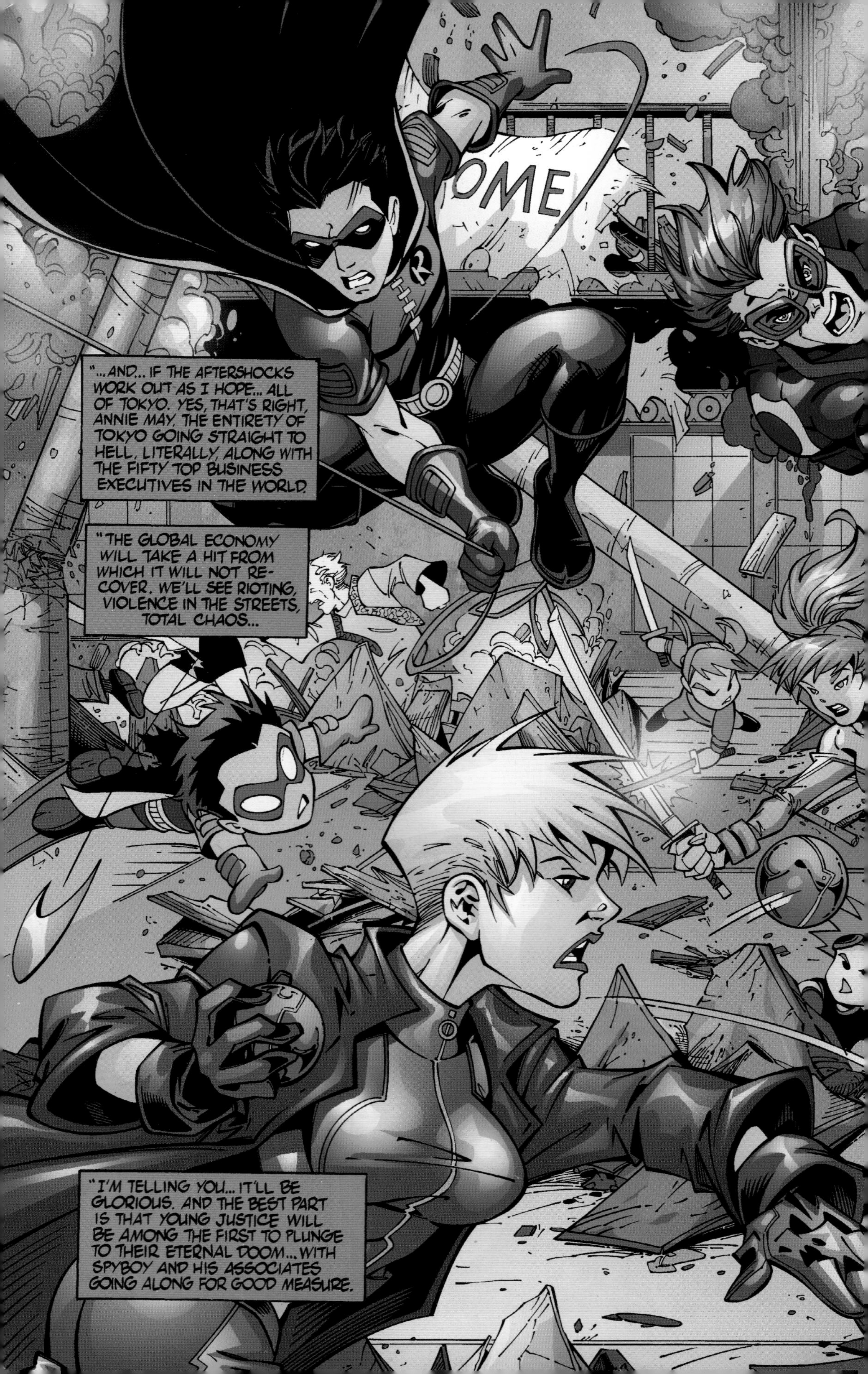
OME
"...AND... IF THE AFTERSHOCKS WORK OUT AS I HOPE... ALL OF TOKYO. YES, THAT'S RIGHT, ANNIE MAY, THE ENTIRETY OF TOKYO GOING STRAIGHT TO HELL, LITERALLY, ALONG WITH THE FIFTY TOP BUSINESS EXECUTIVES IN THE WORLD.
"THE GLOBAL ECONOMY WILL TAKE A HIT FROM WHICH IT WILL NOT RE-COVER. WE'LL SEE RIOTING, VIOLENCE IN THE STREETS, TOTAL CHAOS...
"I'M TELLING YOU... IT'LL BE GLORIOUS. AND THE BEST PART IS THAT YOUNG JUSTICE WILL BE AMONG THE FIRST TO PLUNGE TO THEIR ETERNAL DOOM... WITH SPYBOY AND HIS ASSOCIATES GOING ALONG FOR GOOD MEASURE.

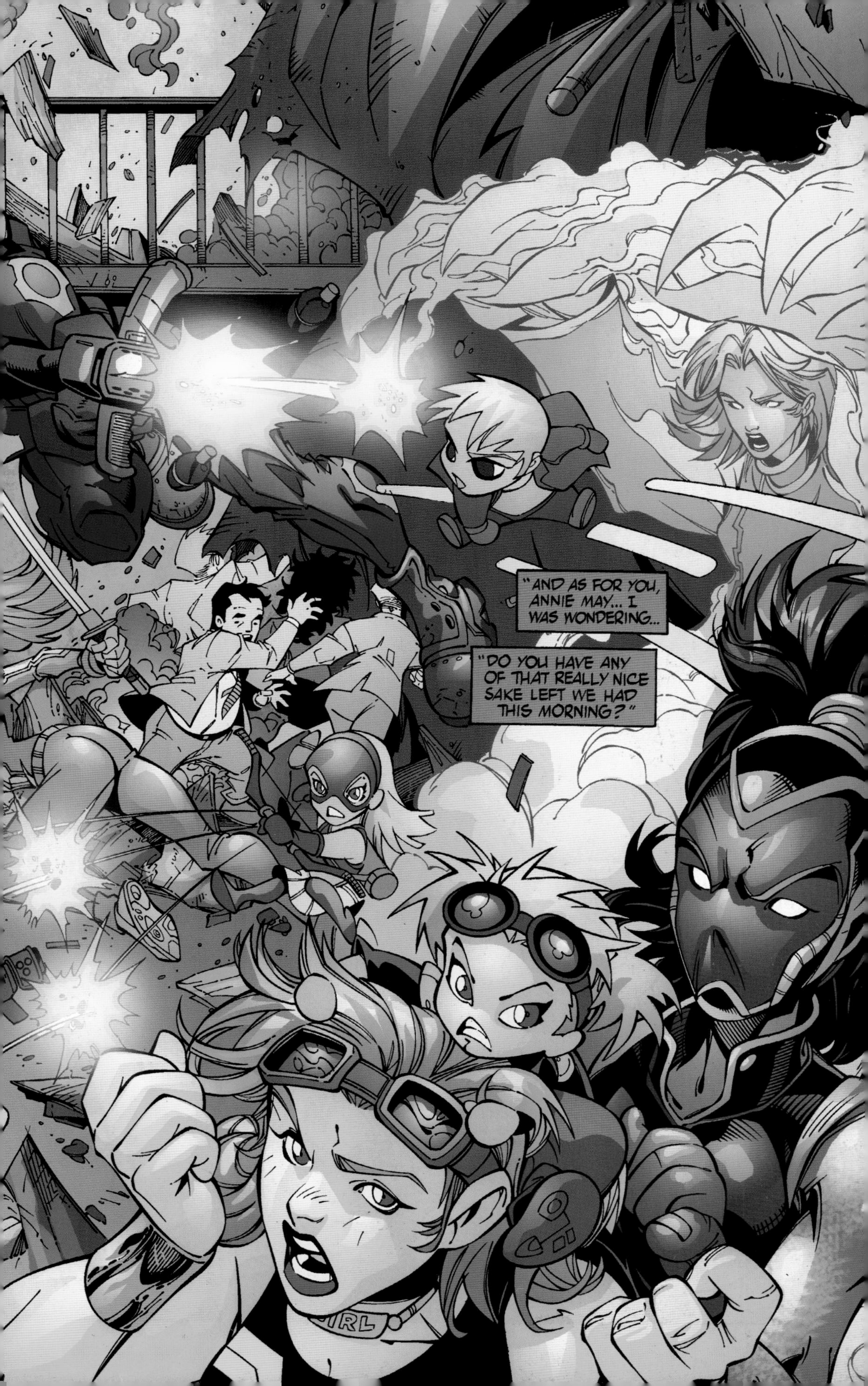
"AND AS FOR YOU, ANNIE MAY... I WAS WONDERING...
"DO YOU HAVE ANY OF THAT REALLY NICE SAKE LEFT WE HAD THIS MORNING?"
GIRL

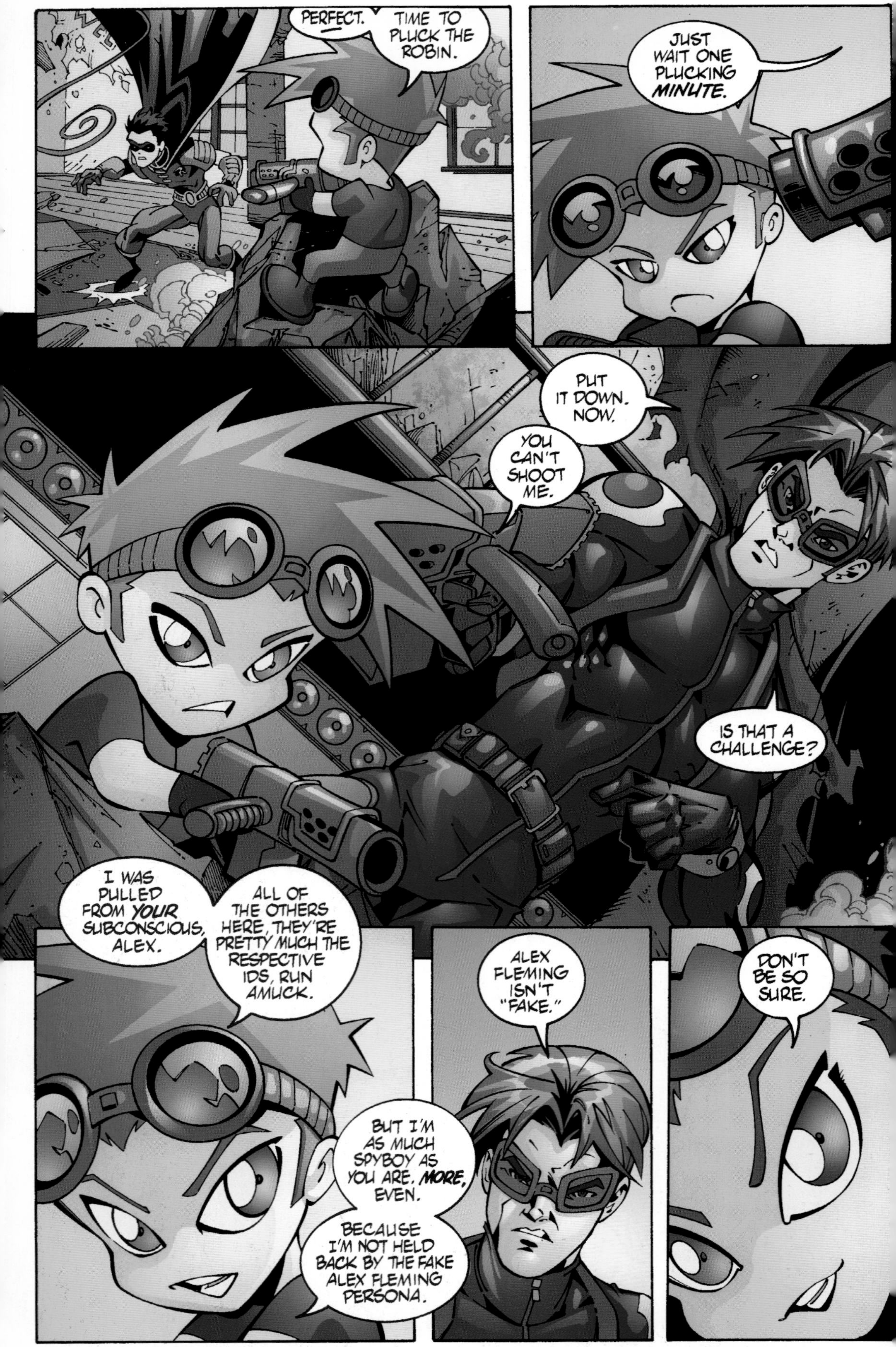
PERFECT.
TIME TO PLUCK THE ROBIN.
JUST WAIT ONE PLUCKING *MINUTE*.
PUT IT DOWN. NOW.
YOU CAN'T SHOOT ME.
IS THAT A CHALLENGE?
I WAS PULLED FROM *YOUR* SUBCONSCIOUS, ALEX.
ALL OF THE OTHERS HERE, THEY'RE PRETTY MUCH THE RESPECTIVE IDS, RUN AMUCK.
BUT I'M AS MUCH SPYBOY AS YOU ARE. *MORE*, EVEN.
BECAUSE I'M NOT HELD BACK BY THE FAKE ALEX FLEMING PERSONA.
ALEX FLEMING ISN'T "FAKE."
DON'T BE SO SURE.

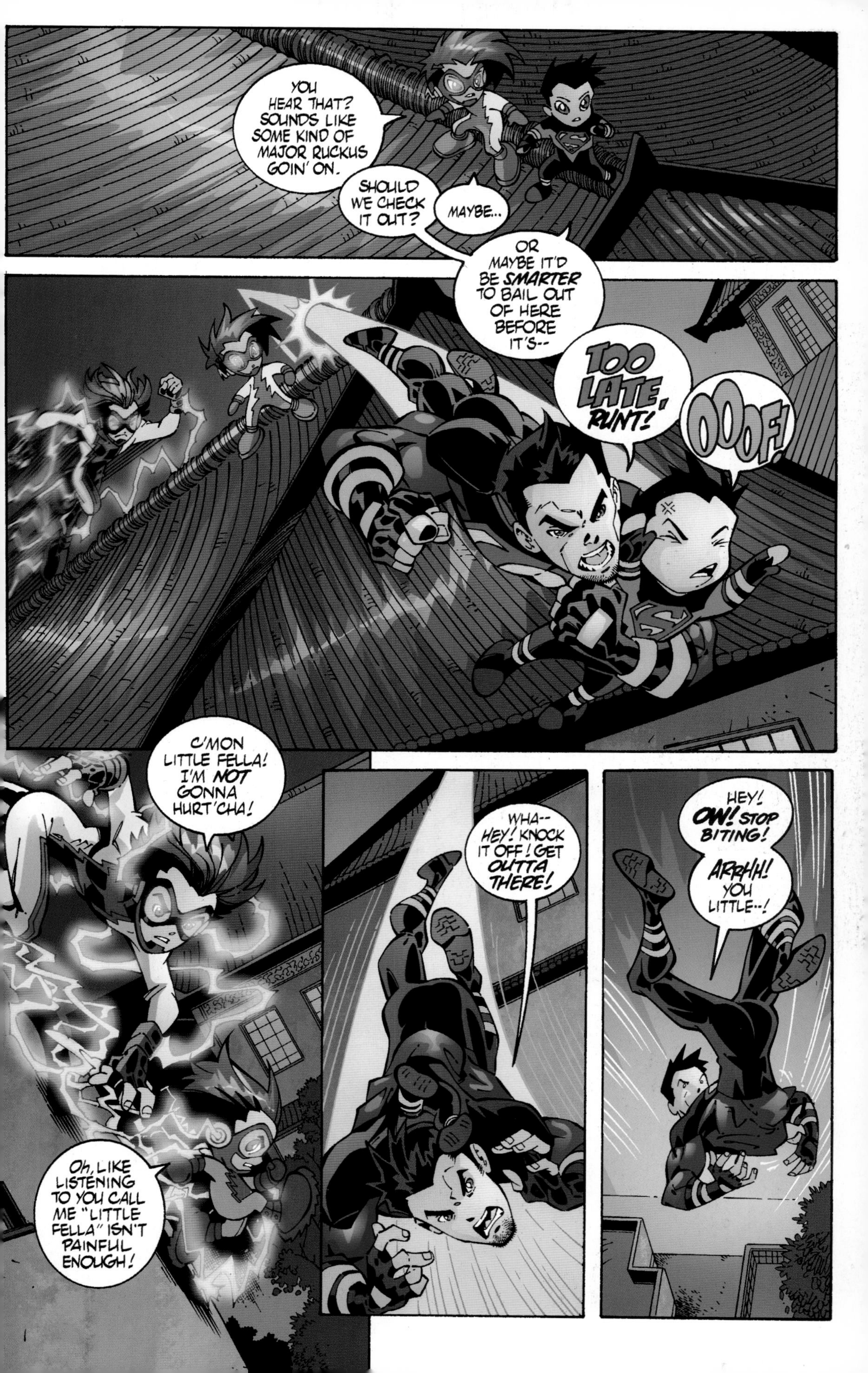
YOU HEAR THAT? SOUNDS LIKE SOME KIND OF MAJOR RUCKUS GOIN' ON.
SHOULD WE CHECK IT OUT?
MAYBE...
OR MAYBE IT'D BE SMARTER TO BAIL OUT OF HERE BEFORE IT'S--
TOO LATE, RUNT!
OOOF!
C'MON LITTLE FELLA! I'M NOT GONNA HURT'CHA!
Oh, LIKE LISTENING TO YOU CALL ME "LITTLE FELLA" ISN'T PAINFUL ENOUGH!
WHA-- HEY! KNOCK IT OFF! GET OUTTA THERE!
HEY! OW! STOP BITING!
ARHH! YOU LITTLE--!

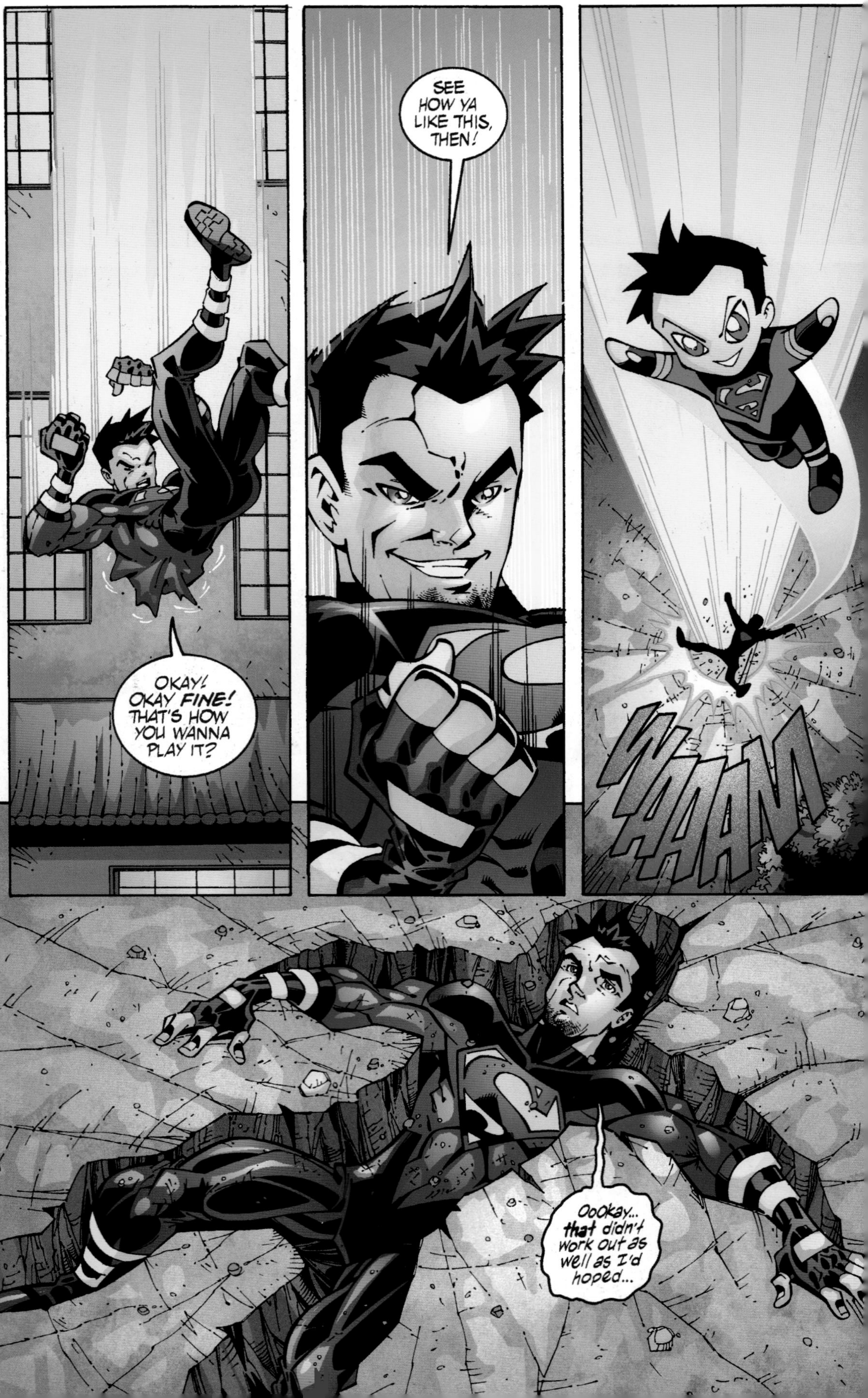
OKAY! OKAY FINE! THAT'S HOW YOU WANNA PLAY IT?
SEE HOW YA LIKE THIS, THEN!
WHAM
Oookay... that didn't work out as well as I'd hoped...

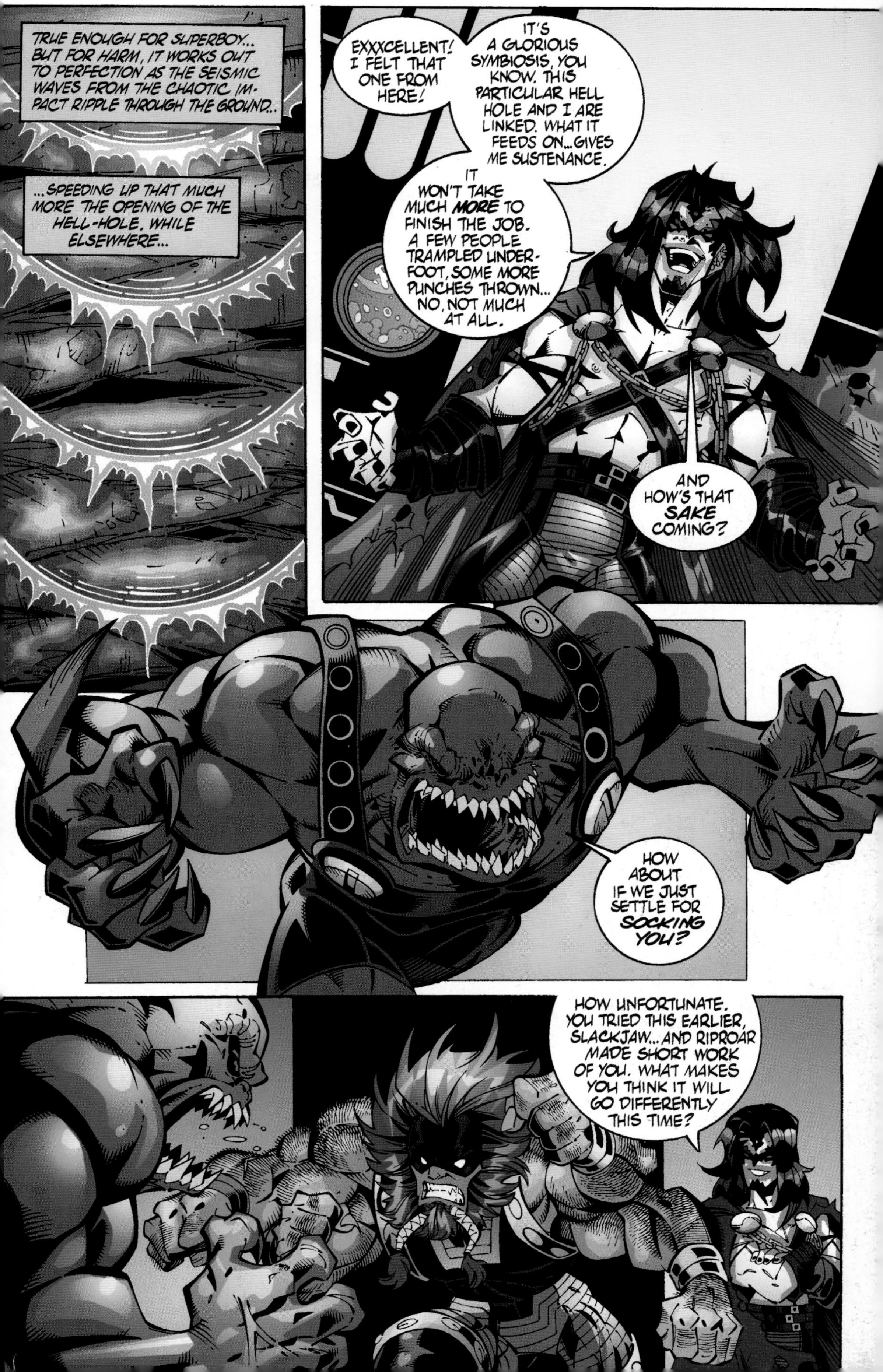
TRUE ENOUGH FOR SUPERBOY... BUT FOR HARM, IT WORKS OUT TO PERFECTION AS THE SEISMIC WAVES FROM THE CHAOTIC IMPACT RIPPLE THROUGH THE GROUND...
...SPEEDING UP THAT MUCH MORE THE OPENING OF THE HELL-HOLE. WHILE ELSEWHERE...
EXXXCELLENT! I FELT THAT ONE FROM HERE!
IT'S A GLORIOUS SYMBIOSIS, YOU KNOW. THIS PARTICULAR HELL HOLE AND I ARE LINKED. WHAT IT FEEDS ON...GIVES ME SUSTENANCE.
IT WON'T TAKE MUCH MORE TO FINISH THE JOB. A FEW PEOPLE TRAMPLED UNDERFOOT, SOME MORE PUNCHES THROWN... NO, NOT MUCH AT ALL.
AND HOW'S THAT SAKE COMING?
HOW ABOUT IF WE JUST SETTLE FOR SOCKING YOU?
HOW UNFORTUNATE. YOU TRIED THIS EARLIER, SLACKJAW... AND RIPROAR MADE SHORT WORK OF YOU. WHAT MAKES YOU THINK IT WILL GO DIFFERENTLY THIS TIME?

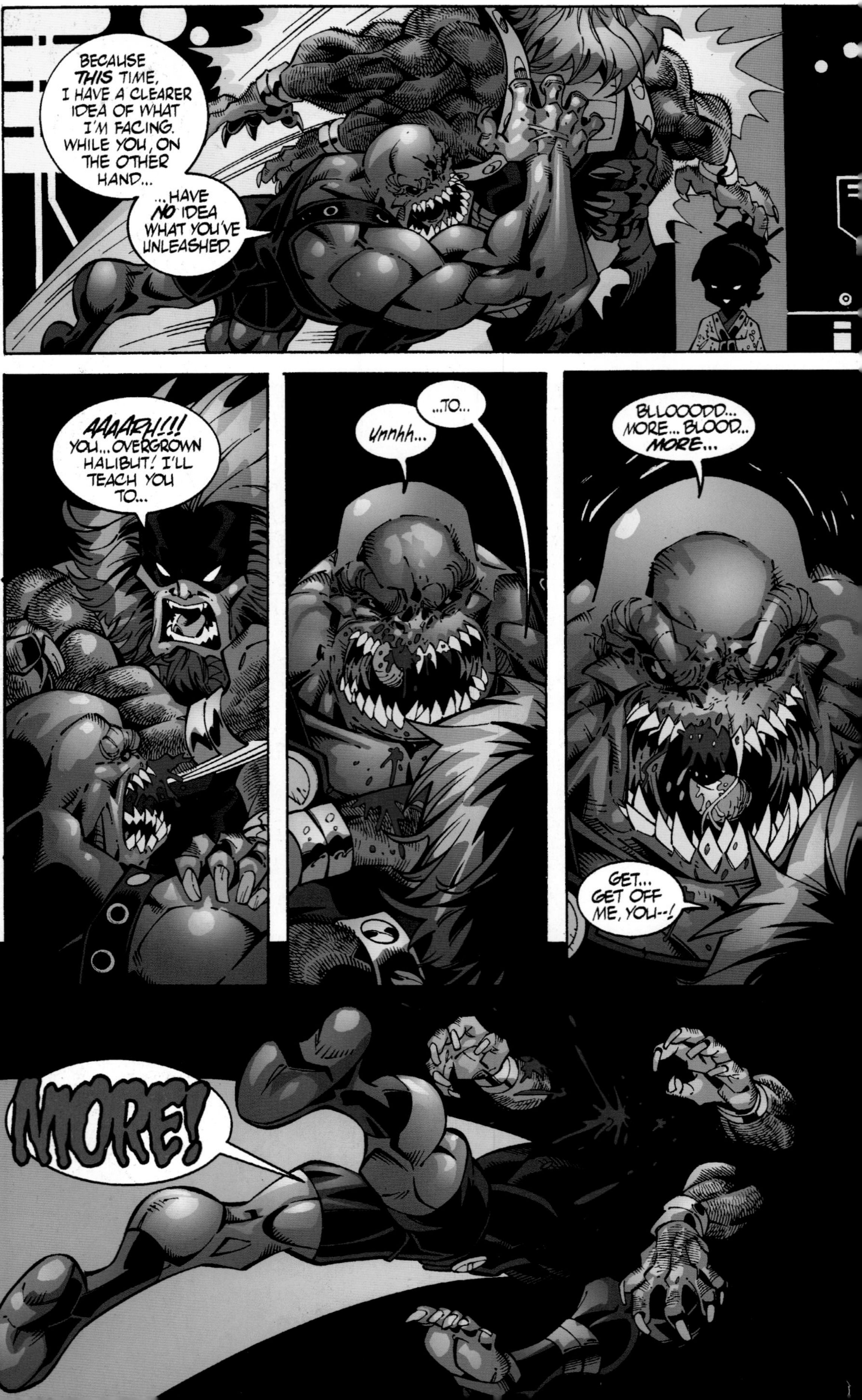
BECAUSE THIS TIME, I HAVE A CLEARER IDEA OF WHAT I'M FACING. WHILE YOU, ON THE OTHER HAND...
...HAVE NO IDEA WHAT YOU'VE UNLEASHED.
AAAARH!!! YOU...OVERGROWN HALIBUT! I'LL TEACH YOU TO...
Unnhh...
...TO...
BLLOOODD... MORE... BLOOD... MORE...
GET... GET OFF ME, YOU--!
MORE!

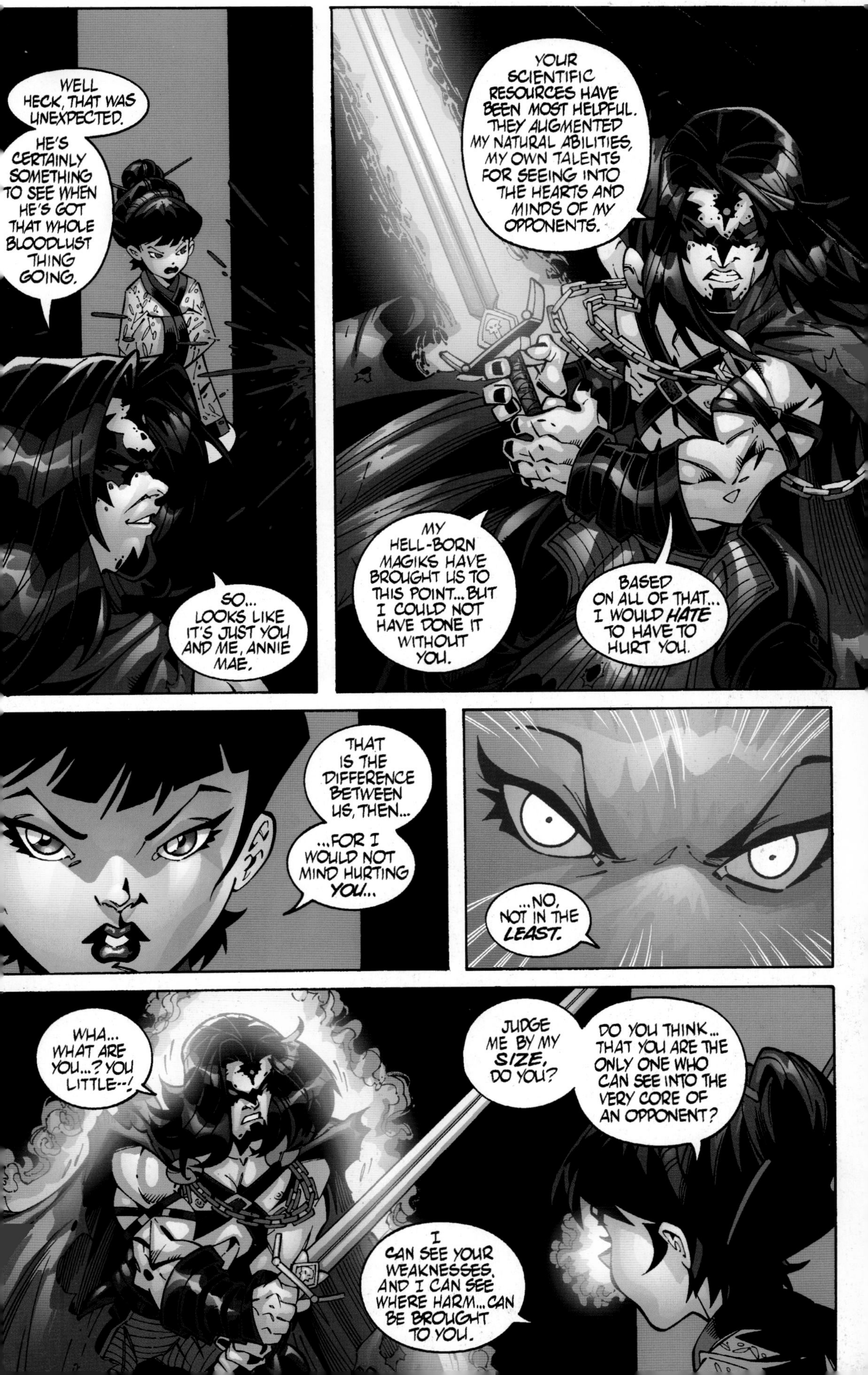
WELL HECK, THAT WAS UNEXPECTED.
HE'S CERTAINLY SOMETHING TO SEE WHEN HE'S GOT THAT WHOLE BLOODLUST THING GOING.
SO... LOOKS LIKE IT'S JUST YOU AND ME, ANNIE MAE.
YOUR SCIENTIFIC RESOURCES HAVE BEEN MOST HELPFUL. THEY AUGMENTED MY NATURAL ABILITIES, MY OWN TALENTS FOR SEEING INTO THE HEARTS AND MINDS OF MY OPPONENTS.
MY HELL-BORN MAGIKS HAVE BROUGHT US TO THIS POINT... BUT I COULD NOT HAVE DONE IT WITHOUT YOU.
BASED ON ALL OF THAT... I WOULD HATE TO HAVE TO HURT YOU.
THAT IS THE DIFFERENCE BETWEEN US, THEN...
...FOR I WOULD NOT MIND HURTING YOU...
...NO, NOT IN THE LEAST.
WHA... WHAT ARE YOU...? YOU LITTLE--!
JUDGE ME BY MY SIZE, DO YOU?
DO YOU THINK... THAT YOU ARE THE ONLY ONE WHO CAN SEE INTO THE VERY CORE OF AN OPPONENT?
I CAN SEE YOUR WEAKNESSES, AND I CAN SEE WHERE HARM... CAN BE BROUGHT TO YOU.

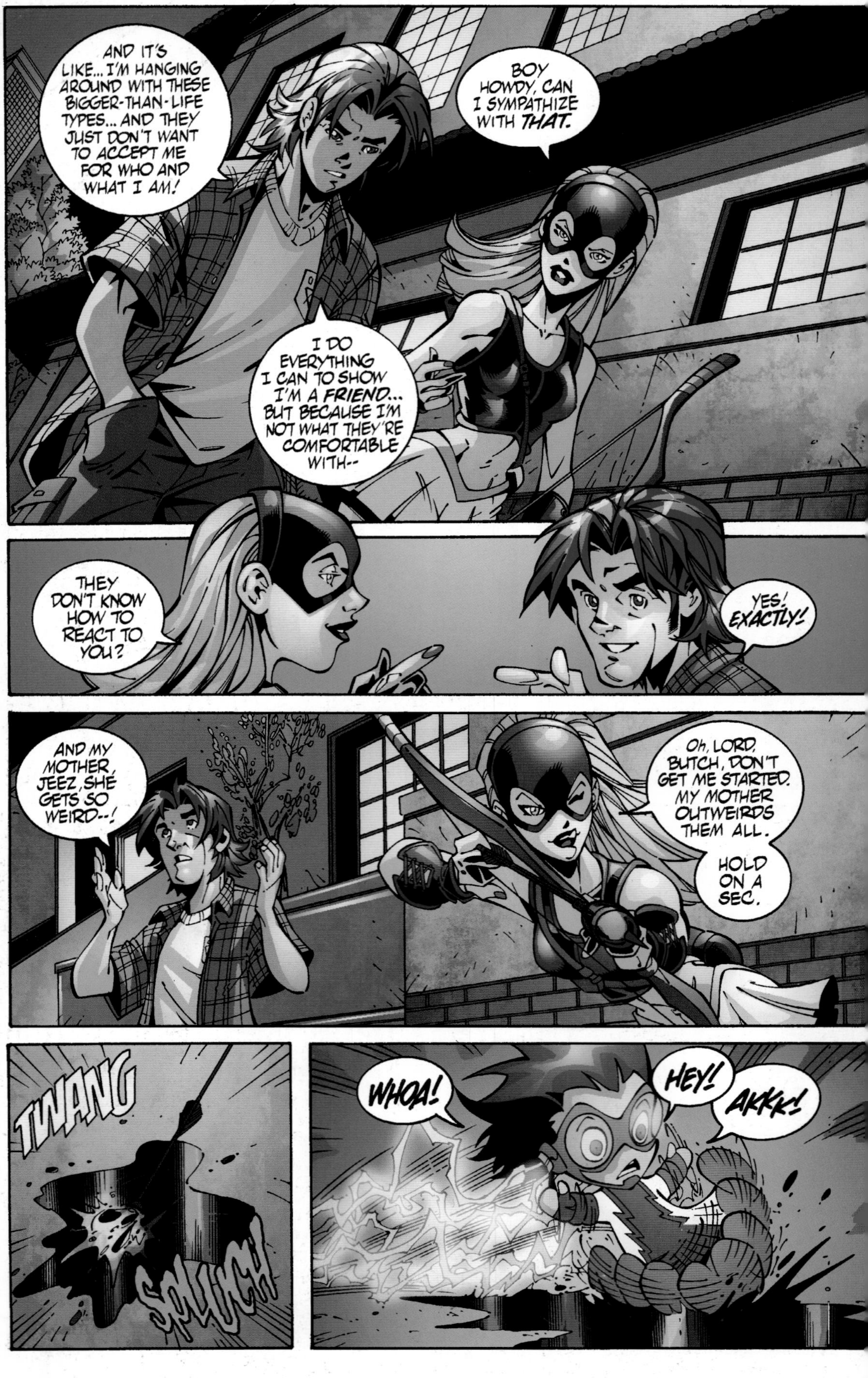

AND IT'S LIKE... I'M HANGING AROUND WITH THESE BIGGER-THAN-LIFE TYPES... AND THEY JUST DON'T WANT TO ACCEPT ME FOR WHO AND WHAT I AM!
BOY HOWDY, CAN I SYMPATHIZE WITH THAT.
I DO EVERYTHING I CAN TO SHOW I'M A FRIEND... BUT BECAUSE I'M NOT WHAT THEY'RE COMFORTABLE WITH--
THEY DON'T KNOW HOW TO REACT TO YOU?
YES! EXACTLY!
AND MY MOTHER, JEEZ, SHE GETS SO WEIRD--!
Oh, LORD, BUTCH, DON'T GET ME STARTED. MY MOTHER OUTWEIRDS THEM ALL.
HOLD ON A SEC.
TWANG
SPLUCH
WHOA!
HEY!
AKKK!

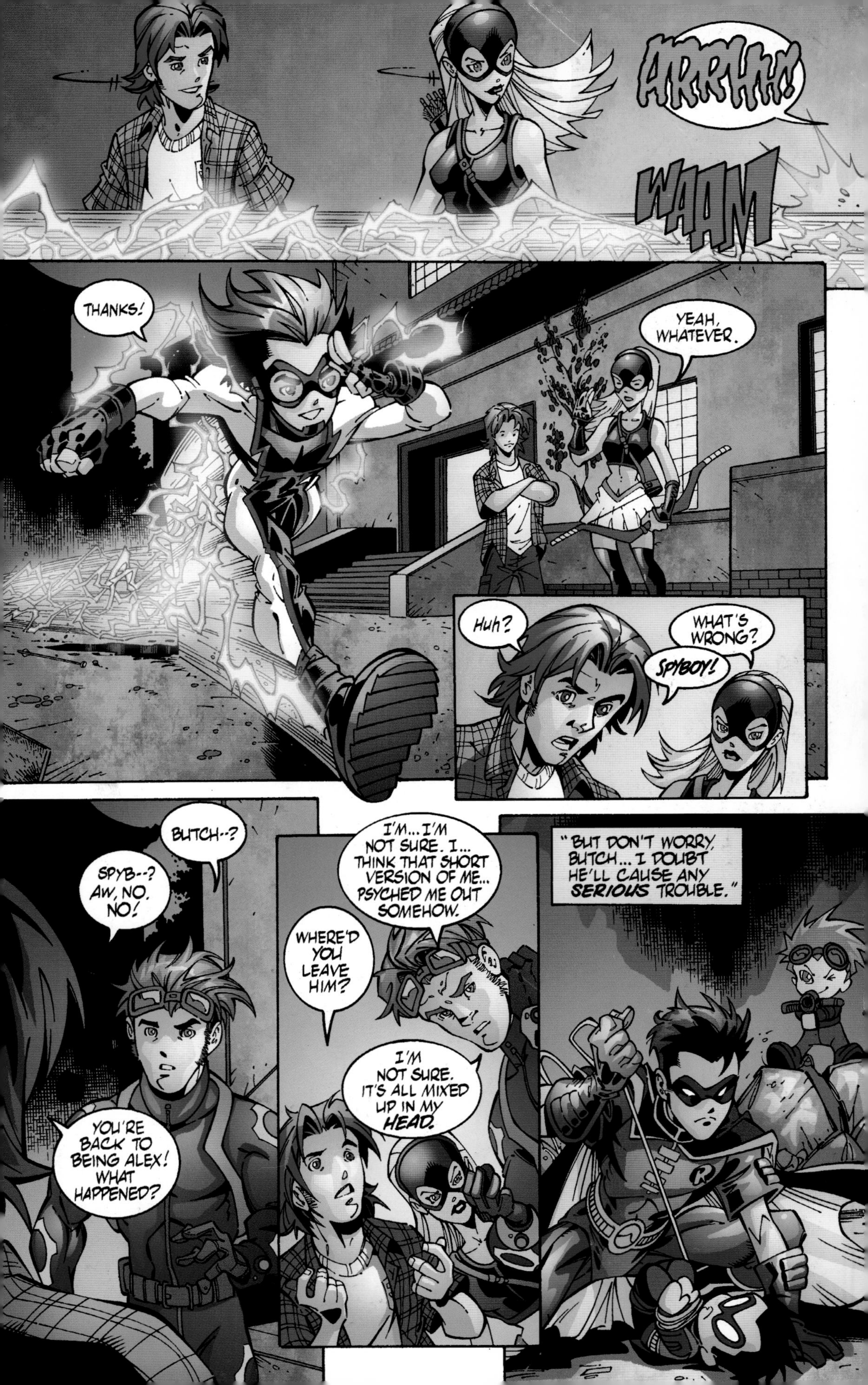
ARRHH!
WAAM
THANKS!
YEAH, WHATEVER.
Huh?
WHAT'S WRONG?
SPYBOY!
BUTCH--?
SPYB--? AW, NO. NO!
YOU'RE BACK TO BEING ALEX! WHAT HAPPENED?
I'M... I'M NOT SURE. I... THINK THAT SHORT VERSION OF ME... PSYCHED ME OUT SOMEHOW.
WHERE'D YOU LEAVE HIM?
I'M NOT SURE. IT'S ALL MIXED UP IN MY HEAD.
"BUT DON'T WORRY, BUTCH... I DOUBT HE'LL CAUSE ANY SERIOUS TROUBLE."

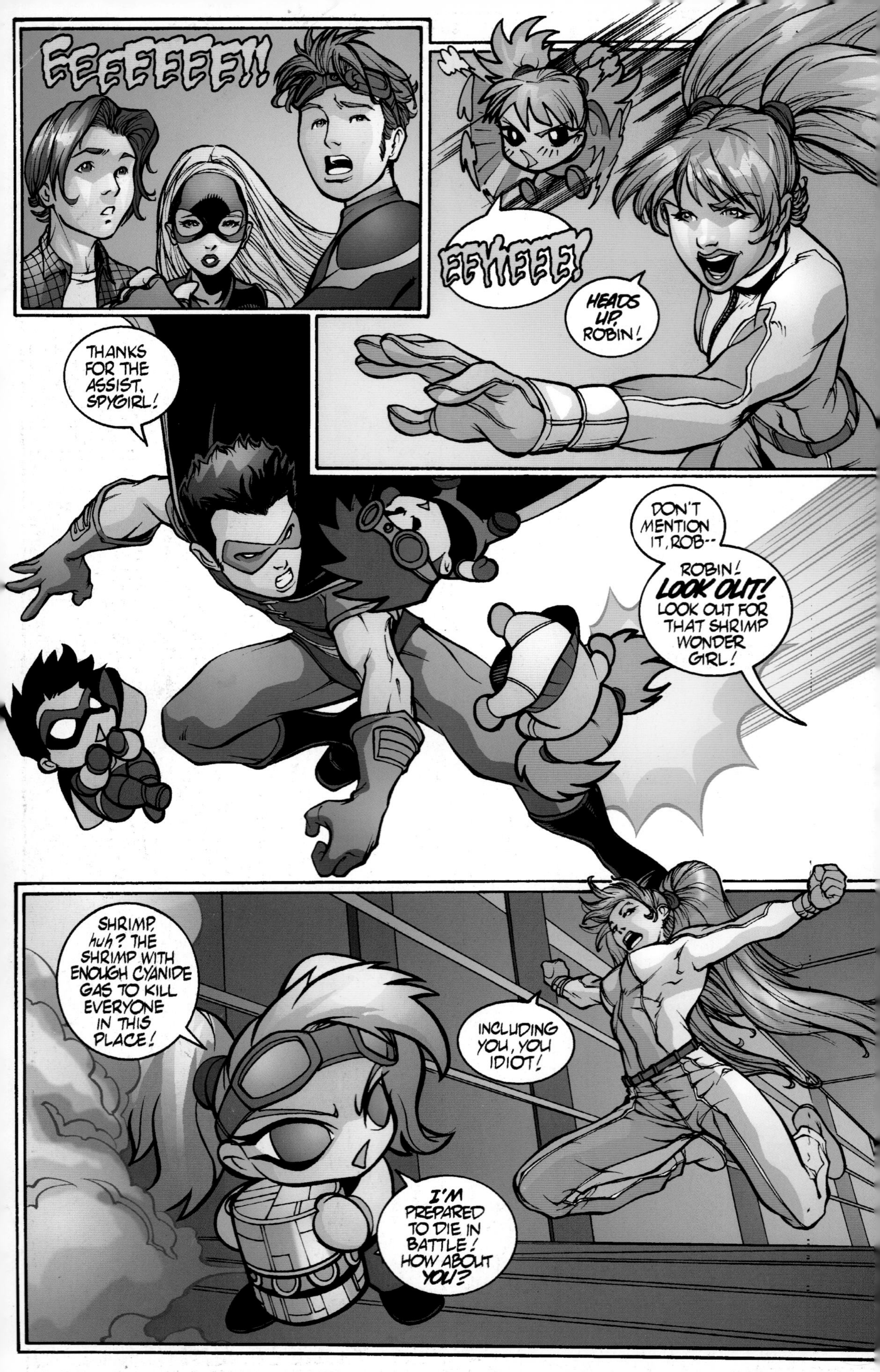
EEEEEEEE!!
EEYEEEE!
HEADS UP, ROBIN!
THANKS FOR THE ASSIST, SPYGIRL!
DON'T MENTION IT, ROB--
ROBIN! LOOK OUT! LOOK OUT FOR THAT SHRIMP WONDER GIRL!
SHRIMP, huh? THE SHRIMP WITH ENOUGH CYANIDE GAS TO KILL EVERYONE IN THIS PLACE!
INCLUDING YOU, YOU IDIOT!
I'M PREPARED TO DIE IN BATTLE! HOW ABOUT YOU?

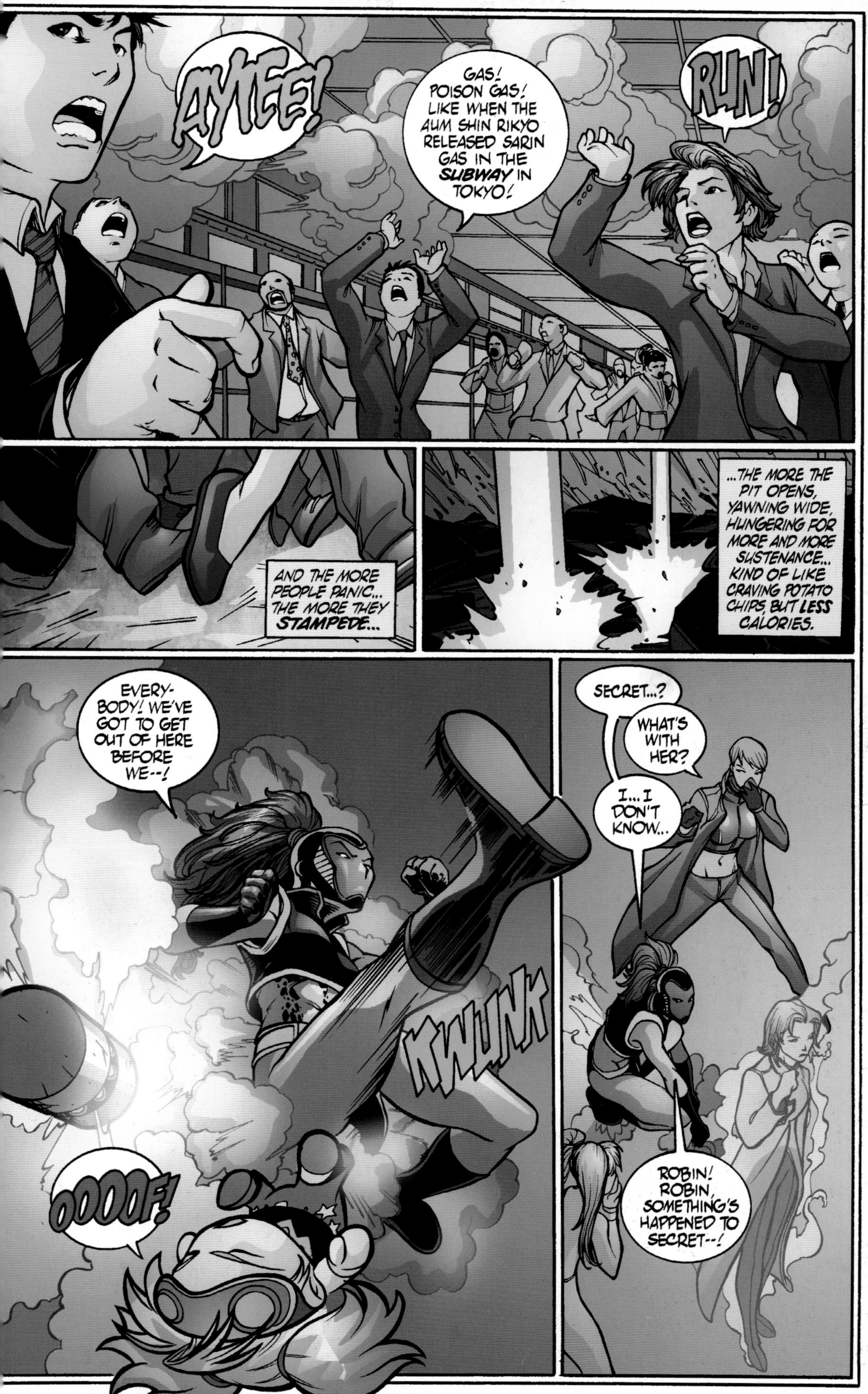
AYIEE!
GAS! POISON GAS! LIKE WHEN THE AUM SHIN RIKYO RELEASED SARIN GAS IN THE SUBWAY IN TOKYO!
RUN!
AND THE MORE PEOPLE PANIC... THE MORE THEY STAMPEDE...
...THE MORE THE PIT OPENS, YAWNING WIDE, HUNGERING FOR MORE AND MORE SUSTENANCE... KIND OF LIKE CRAVING POTATO CHIPS, BUT LESS CALORIES.
EVERY-BODY! WE'VE GOT TO GET OUT OF HERE BEFORE WE--!
KWUNK
OOOOF!
SECRET...?
WHAT'S WITH HER?
I... I DON'T KNOW...
ROBIN! ROBIN, SOMETHING'S HAPPENED TO SECRET--!

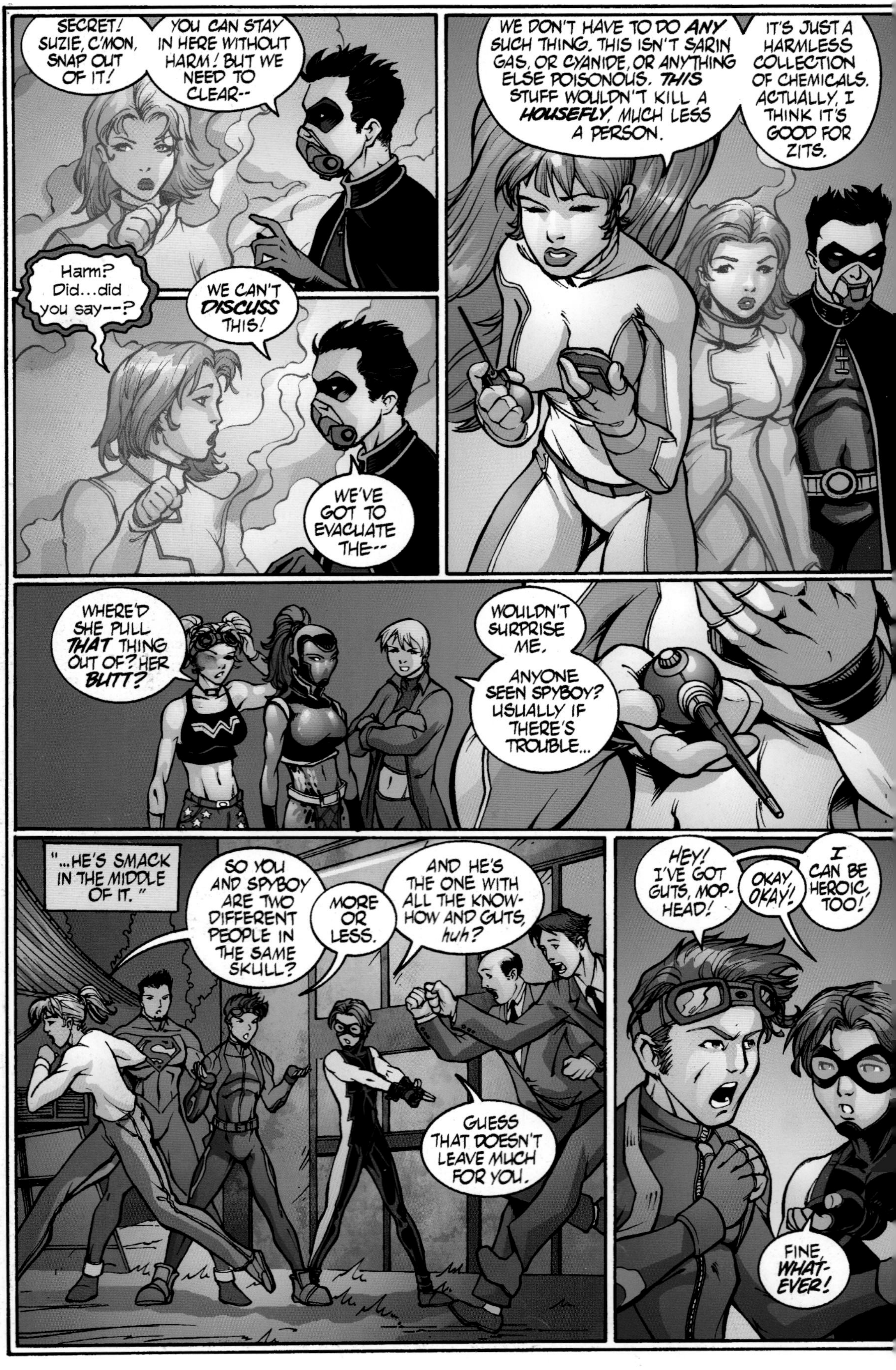
SECRET! SUZIE, C'MON, SNAP OUT OF IT!
YOU CAN STAY IN HERE WITHOUT HARM! BUT WE NEED TO CLEAR--
Harm? Did...did you say--?
WE CAN'T DISCUSS THIS!
WE'VE GOT TO EVACUATE THE--
WE DON'T HAVE TO DO ANY SUCH THING. THIS ISN'T SARIN GAS, OR CYANIDE, OR ANYTHING ELSE POISONOUS. THIS STUFF WOULDN'T KILL A HOUSEFLY, MUCH LESS A PERSON.
IT'S JUST A HARMLESS COLLECTION OF CHEMICALS. ACTUALLY, I THINK IT'S GOOD FOR ZITS.
WHERE'D SHE PULL THAT THING OUT OF? HER BUTT?
WOULDN'T SURPRISE ME.
ANYONE SEEN SPYBOY? USUALLY IF THERE'S TROUBLE...
"...HE'S SMACK IN THE MIDDLE OF IT."
SO YOU AND SPYBOY ARE TWO DIFFERENT PEOPLE IN THE SAME SKULL?
MORE OR LESS.
AND HE'S THE ONE WITH ALL THE KNOW-HOW AND GUTS, huh?
GUESS THAT DOESN'T LEAVE MUCH FOR YOU.
HEY! I'VE GOT GUTS, MOP-HEAD!
OKAY, OKAY!
I CAN BE HEROIC, TOO!
FINE. WHAT-EVER!

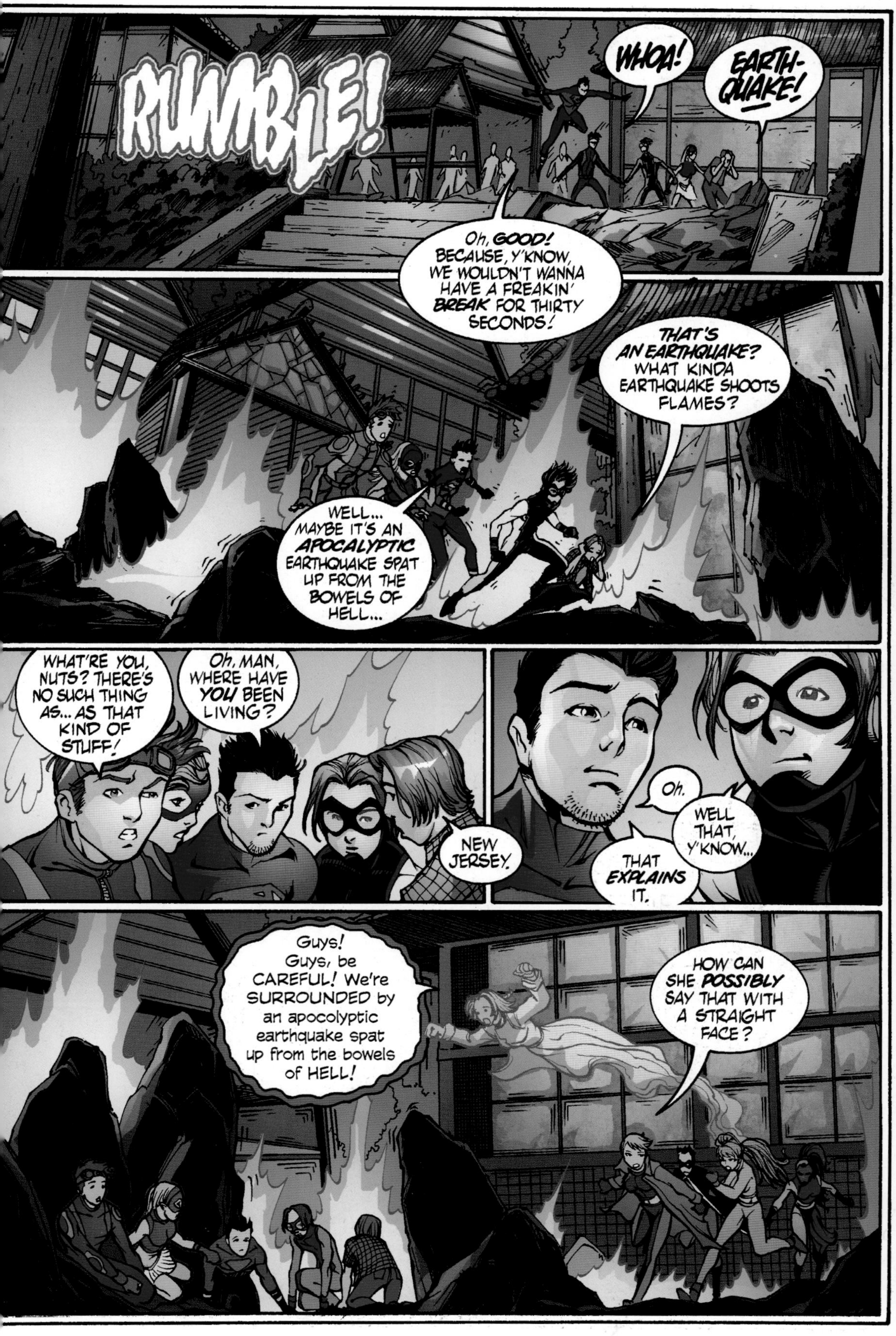
RUMBLE!
WHOA!
EARTH-QUAKE!
Oh, GOOD! BECAUSE, Y'KNOW, WE WOULDN'T WANNA HAVE A FREAKIN' BREAK FOR THIRTY SECONDS!
THAT'S AN EARTHQUAKE? WHAT KINDA EARTHQUAKE SHOOTS FLAMES?
WELL... MAYBE IT'S AN APOCALYPTIC EARTHQUAKE SPAT UP FROM THE BOWELS OF HELL...
WHAT'RE YOU, NUTS? THERE'S NO SUCH THING AS... AS THAT KIND OF STUFF!
Oh, MAN, WHERE HAVE YOU BEEN LIVING?
NEW JERSEY.
Oh.
WELL THAT, Y'KNOW...
THAT EXPLAINS IT.
Guys! Guys, be CAREFUL! We're SURROUNDED by an apocolyptic earthquake spat up from the bowels of HELL!
HOW CAN SHE POSSIBLY SAY THAT WITH A STRAIGHT FACE?

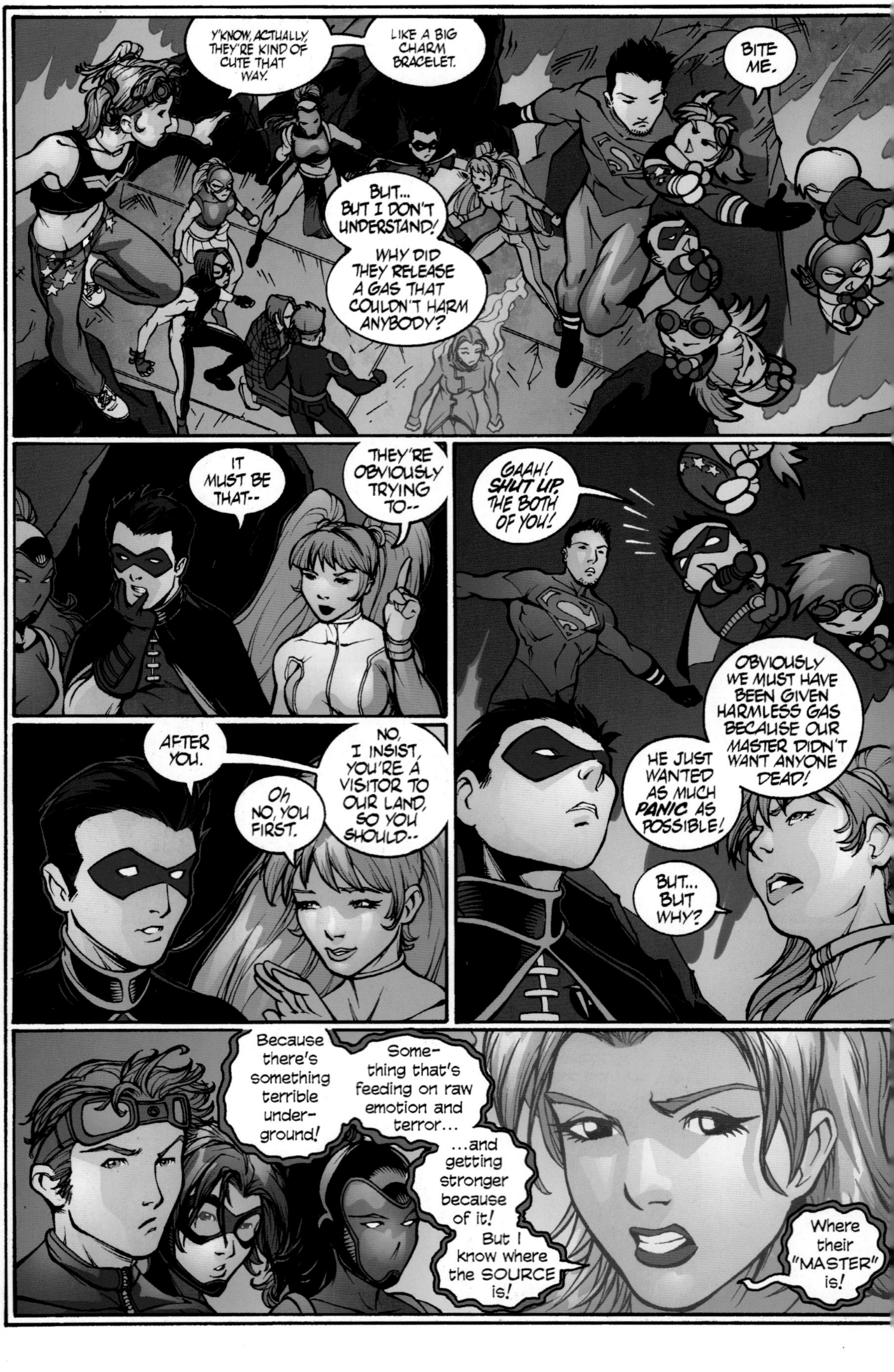
Y'KNOW, ACTUALLY, THEY'RE KIND OF CUTE THAT WAY.
LIKE A BIG CHARM BRACELET.
BITE ME.
BUT... BUT I DON'T UNDERSTAND!
WHY DID THEY RELEASE A GAS THAT COULDN'T HARM ANYBODY?
IT MUST BE THAT--
THEY'RE OBVIOUSLY TRYING TO--
AFTER YOU.
NO, I INSIST, YOU'RE A VISITOR TO OUR LAND, SO YOU SHOULD--
Oh NO, YOU FIRST.
GAAH! SHUT UP, THE BOTH OF YOU!
OBVIOUSLY WE MUST HAVE BEEN GIVEN HARMLESS GAS BECAUSE OUR MASTER DIDN'T WANT ANYONE DEAD!
HE JUST WANTED AS MUCH PANIC AS POSSIBLE!
BUT... BUT WHY?
Because there's something terrible under-ground!
Some-thing that's feeding on raw emotion and terror...
...and getting stronger because of it!
But I know where the SOURCE is!
Where their "MASTER" is!

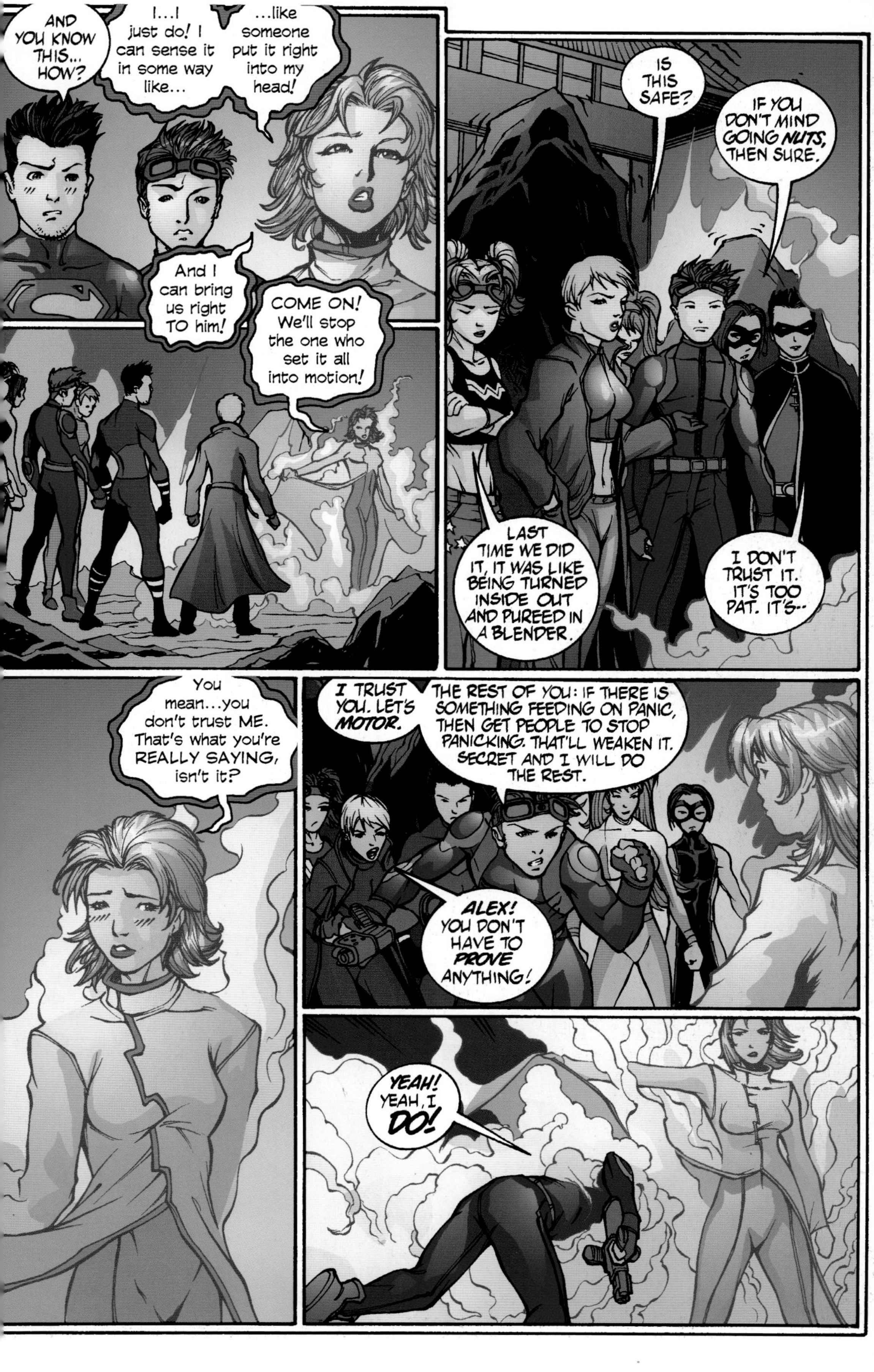
AND YOU KNOW THIS... HOW?
I...I just do! I can sense it in some way like...
...like someone put it right into my head!
And I can bring us right TO him!
COME ON! We'll stop the one who set it all into motion!
IS THIS SAFE?
IF YOU DON'T MIND GOING NUTS, THEN SURE.
LAST TIME WE DID IT, IT WAS LIKE BEING TURNED INSIDE OUT AND PUREED IN A BLENDER.
I DON'T TRUST IT. IT'S TOO PAT. IT'S--
You mean...you don't trust ME. That's what you're REALLY SAYING, isn't it?
I TRUST YOU. LET'S MOTOR.
THE REST OF YOU: IF THERE IS SOMETHING FEEDING ON PANIC, THEN GET PEOPLE TO STOP PANICKING. THAT'LL WEAKEN IT. SECRET AND I WILL DO THE REST.
ALEX! YOU DON'T HAVE TO PROVE ANYTHING!
YEAH! YEAH, I DO!

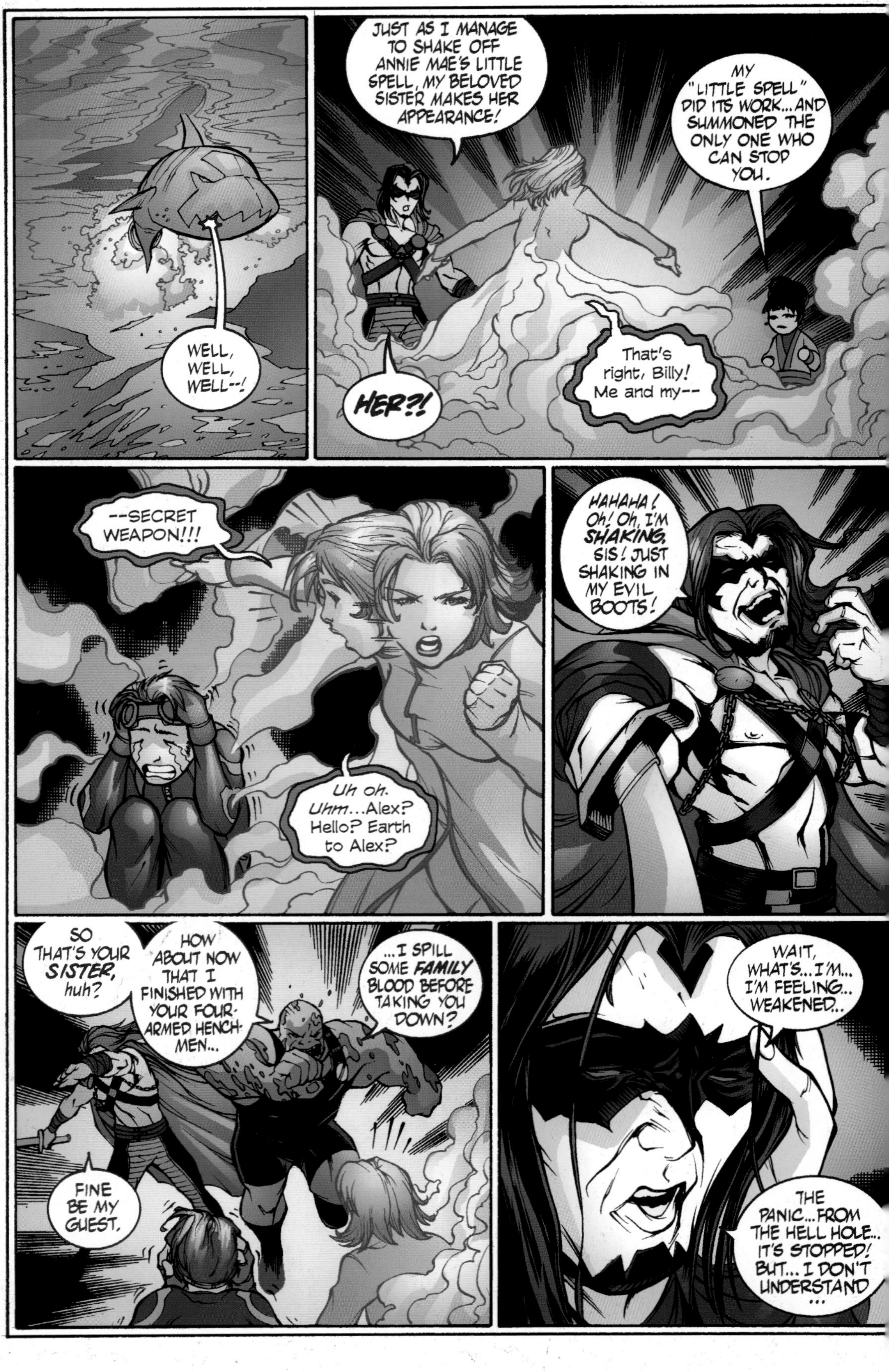
WELL, WELL, WELL--!
JUST AS I MANAGE TO SHAKE OFF ANNIE MAE'S LITTLE SPELL, MY BELOVED SISTER MAKES HER APPEARANCE!
MY "LITTLE SPELL" DID ITS WORK... AND SUMMONED THE ONLY ONE WHO CAN STOP YOU.
HER?!
That's right, Billy! Me and my--
--SECRET WEAPON!!!
Uh oh. Uhm...Alex? Hello? Earth to Alex?
HAHAHA! Oh! Oh, I'M SHAKING, SIS! JUST SHAKING IN MY EVIL BOOTS!
SO THAT'S YOUR SISTER, huh?
HOW ABOUT NOW THAT I FINISHED WITH YOUR FOUR-ARMED HENCH-MEN...
...I SPILL SOME FAMILY BLOOD BEFORE TAKING YOU DOWN?
FINE BE MY GUEST.
WAIT, WHAT'S... I'M... I'M FEELING... WEAKENED...
THE PANIC... FROM THE HELL HOLE... IT'S STOPPED! BUT... I DON'T UNDERSTAND ...

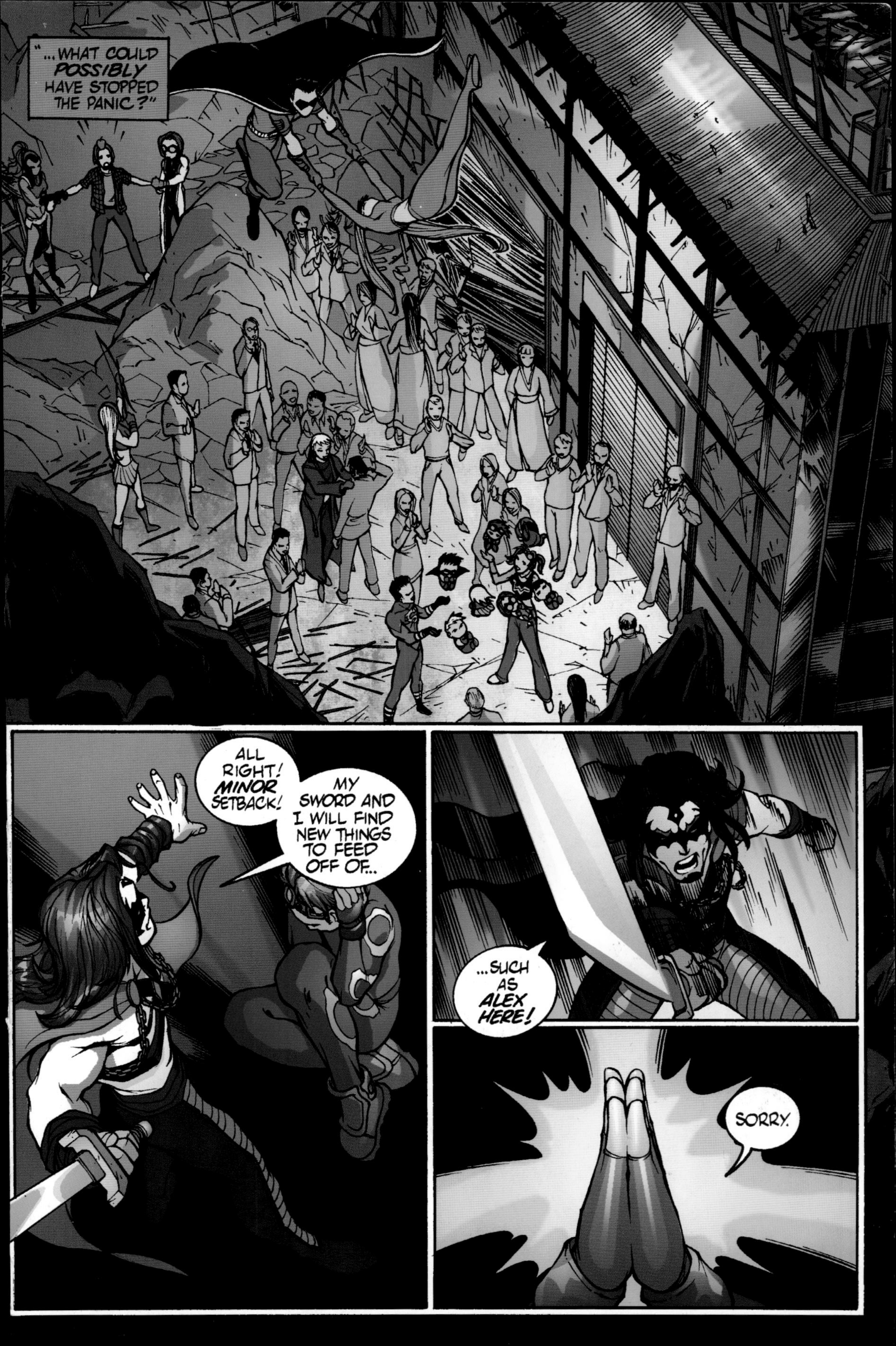
"...WHAT COULD POSSIBLY HAVE STOPPED THE PANIC?"
ALL RIGHT! MINOR SETBACK!
MY SWORD AND I WILL FIND NEW THINGS TO FEED OFF OF...
...SUCH AS ALEX HERE!
SORRY.

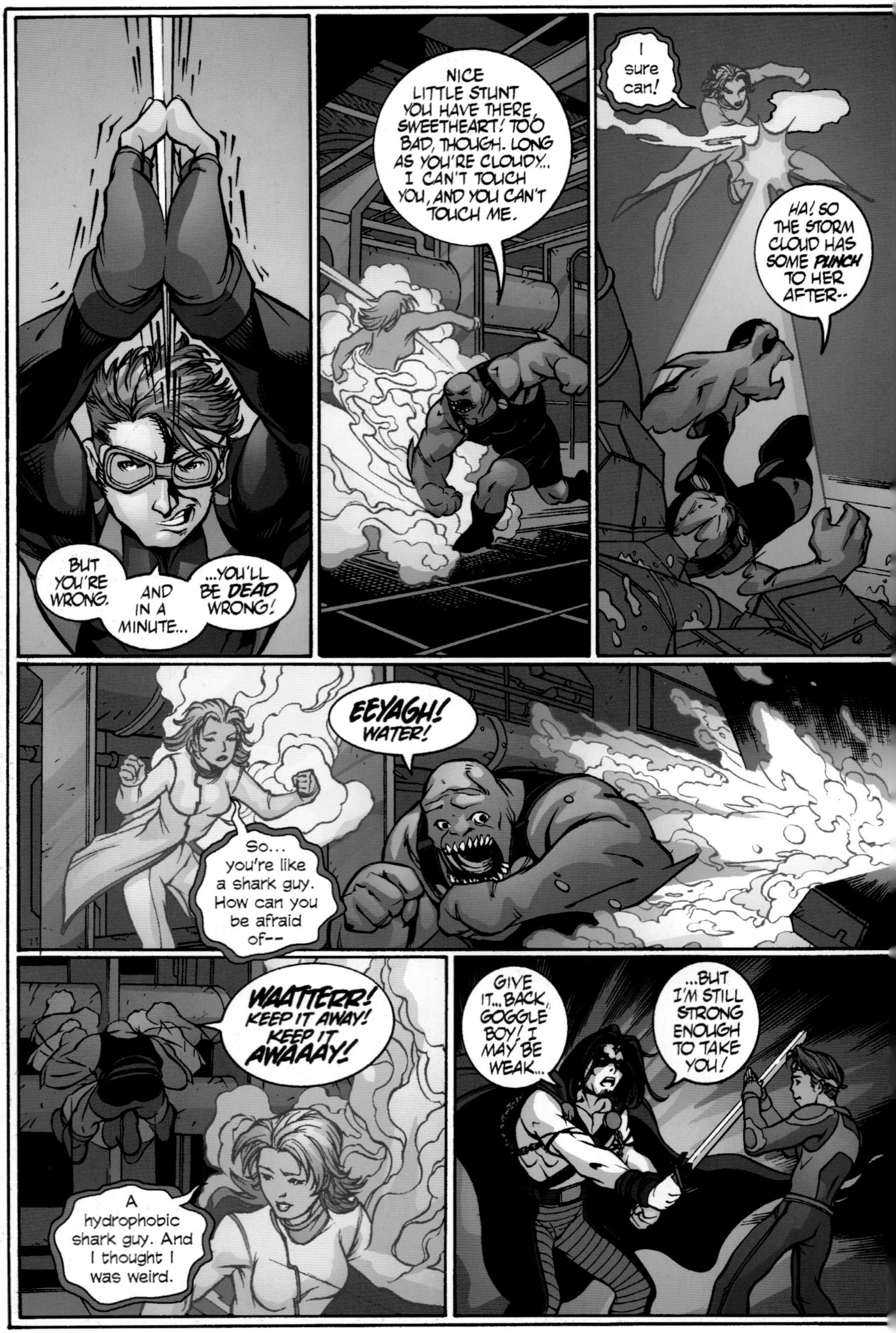
BUT YOU'RE WRONG.
AND IN A MINUTE...
...YOU'LL BE DEAD WRONG!
NICE LITTLE STUNT YOU HAVE THERE, SWEETHEART! TOO BAD, THOUGH. LONG AS YOU'RE CLOUDY... I CAN'T TOUCH YOU, AND YOU CAN'T TOUCH ME.
I sure can!
HA! SO THE STORM CLOUD HAS SOME PUNCH TO HER AFTER--
EEYAGH! WATER!
So... you're like a shark guy. How can you be afraid of--
WAATTERR! KEEP IT AWAY! KEEP IT AWAAAY!
A hydrophobic shark guy. And I thought I was weird.
GIVE IT... BACK, GOGGLE BOY! I MAY BE WEAK...
...BUT I'M STILL STRONG ENOUGH TO TAKE YOU!

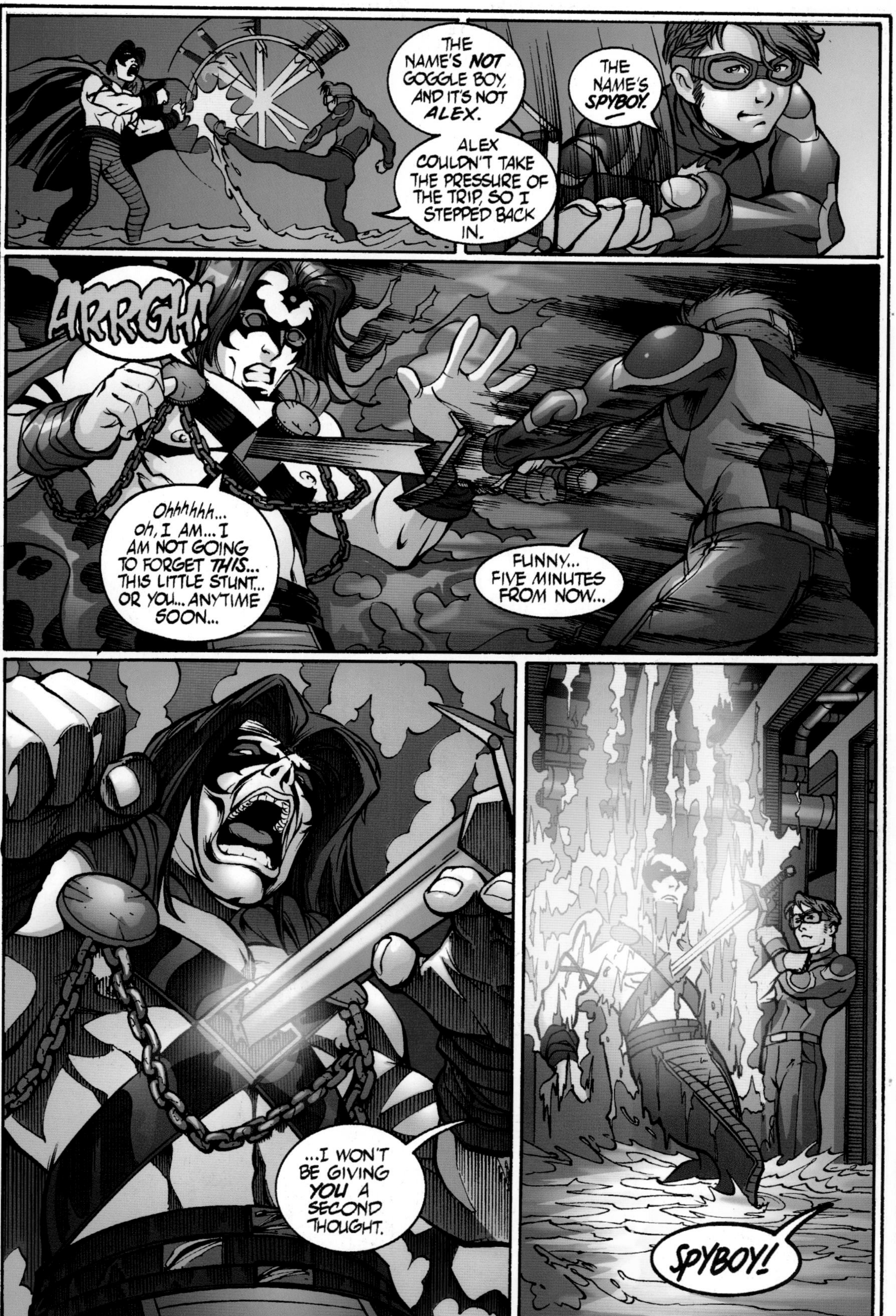
THE NAME'S **NOT** GOGGLE BOY, AND IT'S NOT **ALEX**.
ALEX COULDN'T TAKE THE PRESSURE OF THE TRIP, SO I STEPPED BACK IN.
THE NAME'S **SPYBOY**.
ARRGH!
Ohhhhhh... oh, I AM... I AM NOT GOING TO FORGET **THIS**... THIS LITTLE STUNT... OR YOU... ANYTIME SOON...
FUNNY... FIVE MINUTES FROM NOW...
...I WON'T BE GIVING **YOU** A SECOND THOUGHT.
SPYBOY!

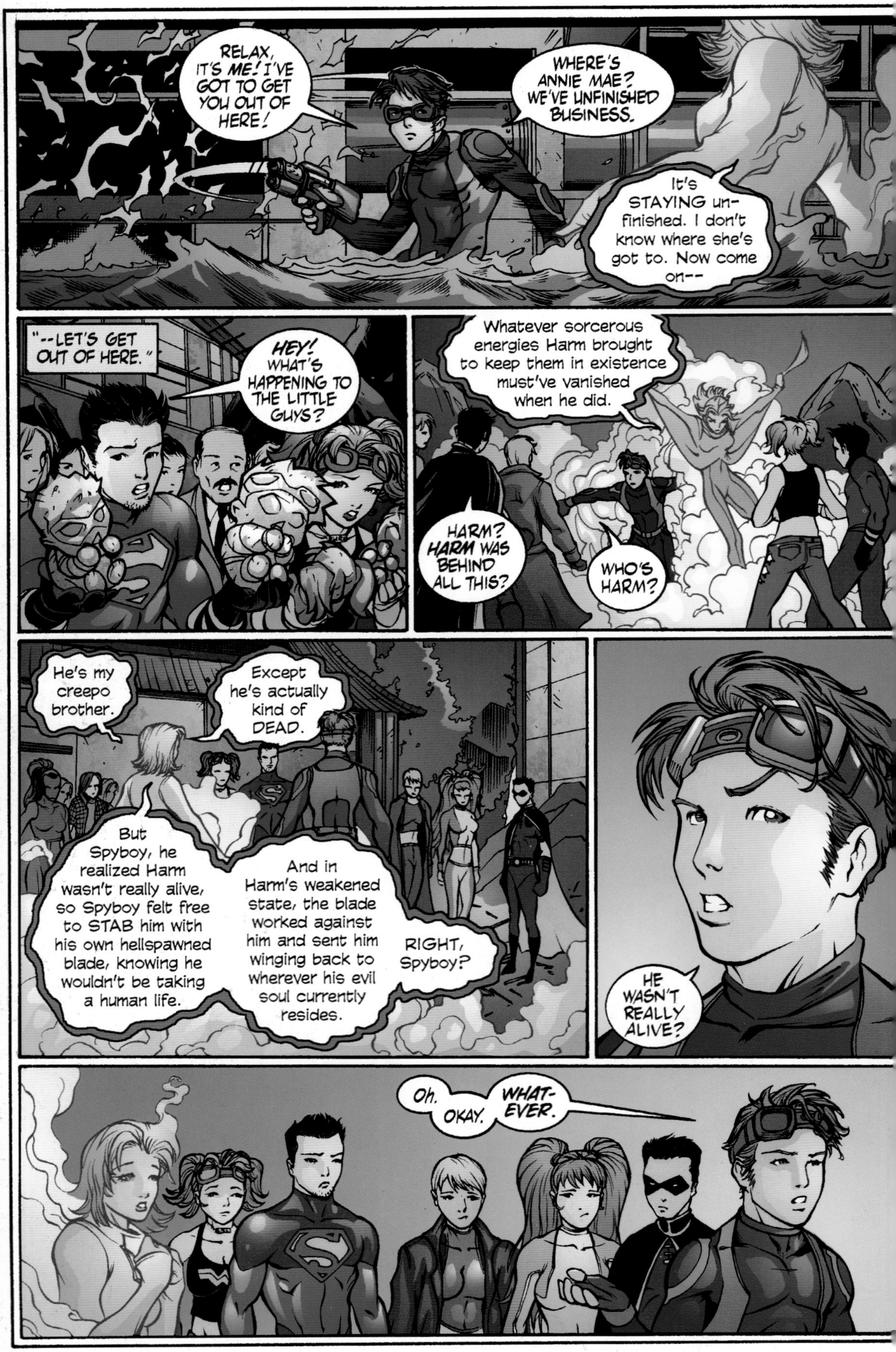
RELAX, IT'S *ME!* I'VE GOT TO GET YOU OUT OF HERE!
WHERE'S ANNIE MAE? WE'VE UNFINISHED BUSINESS.
It's STAYING unfinished. I don't know where she's got to. Now come on--
"--LET'S GET OUT OF HERE."
HEY! WHAT'S HAPPENING TO THE LITTLE GUYS?
Whatever sorcerous energies Harm brought to keep them in existence must've vanished when he did.
HARM? *HARM* WAS BEHIND ALL THIS?
WHO'S HARM?
He's my creepo brother.
Except he's actually kind of DEAD.
But Spyboy, he realized Harm wasn't really alive, so Spyboy felt free to STAB him with his own hellspawned blade, knowing he wouldn't be taking a human life.
And in Harm's weakened state, the blade worked against him and sent him winging back to wherever his evil soul currently resides.
RIGHT, Spyboy?
HE WASN'T REALLY ALIVE?
Oh.
OKAY.
WHAT-EVER.

END

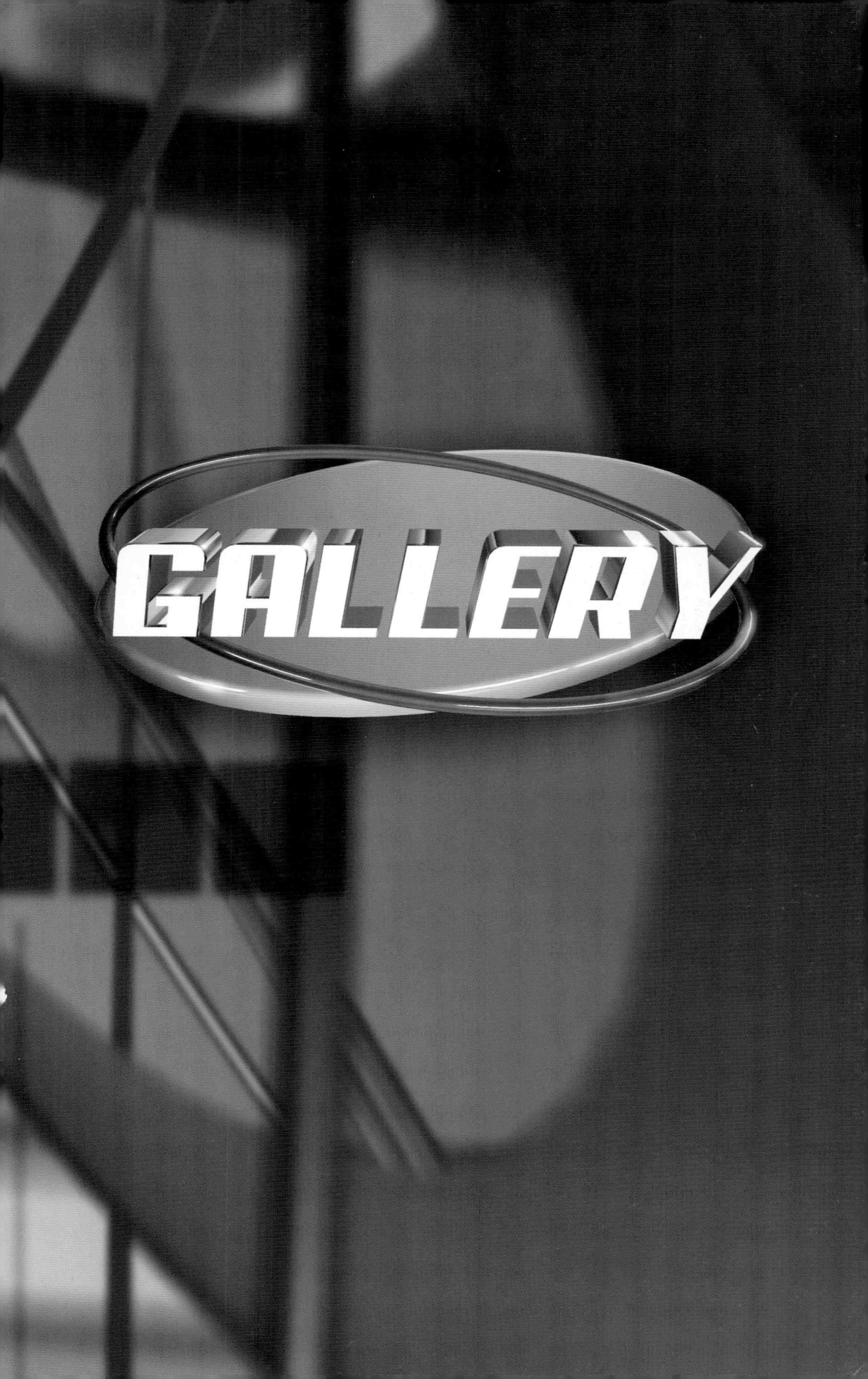
GALLERY

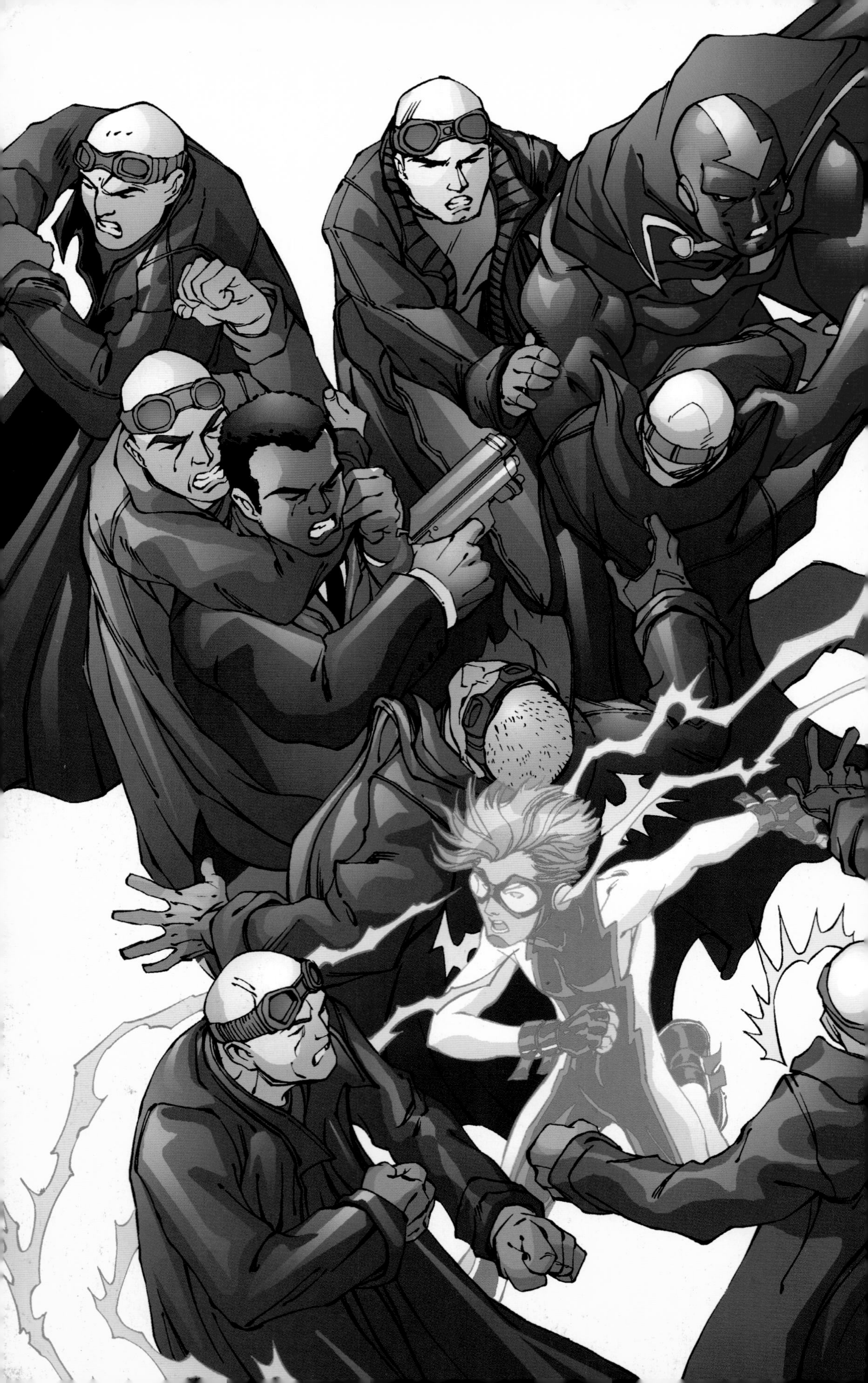

CROSS ON OVER!

DON'T MISS THESE GREAT CROSSOVER TITLES FROM DARK HORSE COMICS AND DC COMICS!

ALIENS
VERSUS
PREDATOR

Aliens vs. Predator
1-56971-125-9
$19.95

ALIENS
VERSUS
PREDATOR
VERSUS
THE TERMINATOR

Aliens vs. Predator vs. The Terminator
1-56971-568-8
$11.95

ALIENS
VERSUS
PREDATOR
eternal
Ian Edginton and Alex Maleev

Aliens vs. Predator: Eternal
1-56971-409-6
$9.95

ALIENS
PREDATOR
WAR
INTRODUCTION BY ROBERT SHECKLEY

Aliens vs. Predator: War
1-56971-158-5
$19.95

MINDHUNTER
PREDATOR
ALIENS

Aliens/Predator/Witchblade/Darkness: Mindhunter
1-56971-615-3
$9.95

ALIENS
PREDATOR
DEADLIEST of the SPECIES
CLAREMONT • GUICE • BARRETO

Aliens/Predator: The Deadliest of the Species
1-56971-184-4
$29.95
Limited Edition Hardcover
1-56971-182-8
$99.95

BATMAN
ALIENS
RON MARZ • BERNIE WRIGHTSON

Batman/Aliens
1-56971-305-7
$14.95

BATMAN
CLAWS OF THE CAT-WOMAN
TARZAN
RON MARZ
IGOR KORDEY

Batman/Tarzan: The Claws of the Catwoman
1-56971-466-5
$10.95

GHOST
BATGIRL
the resurrection engine

Ghost/Batgirl: The Resurrection Engine
1-56971-570-X
$11.95

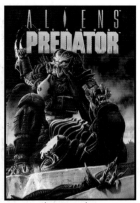

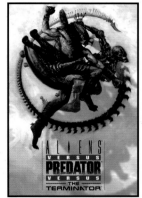

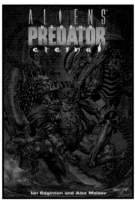

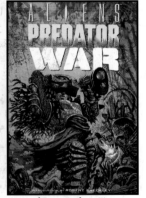

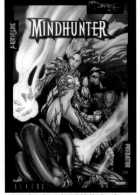

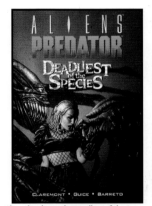

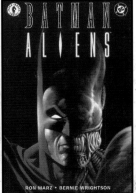

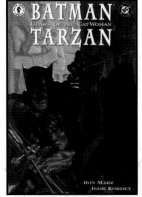

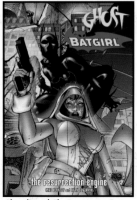

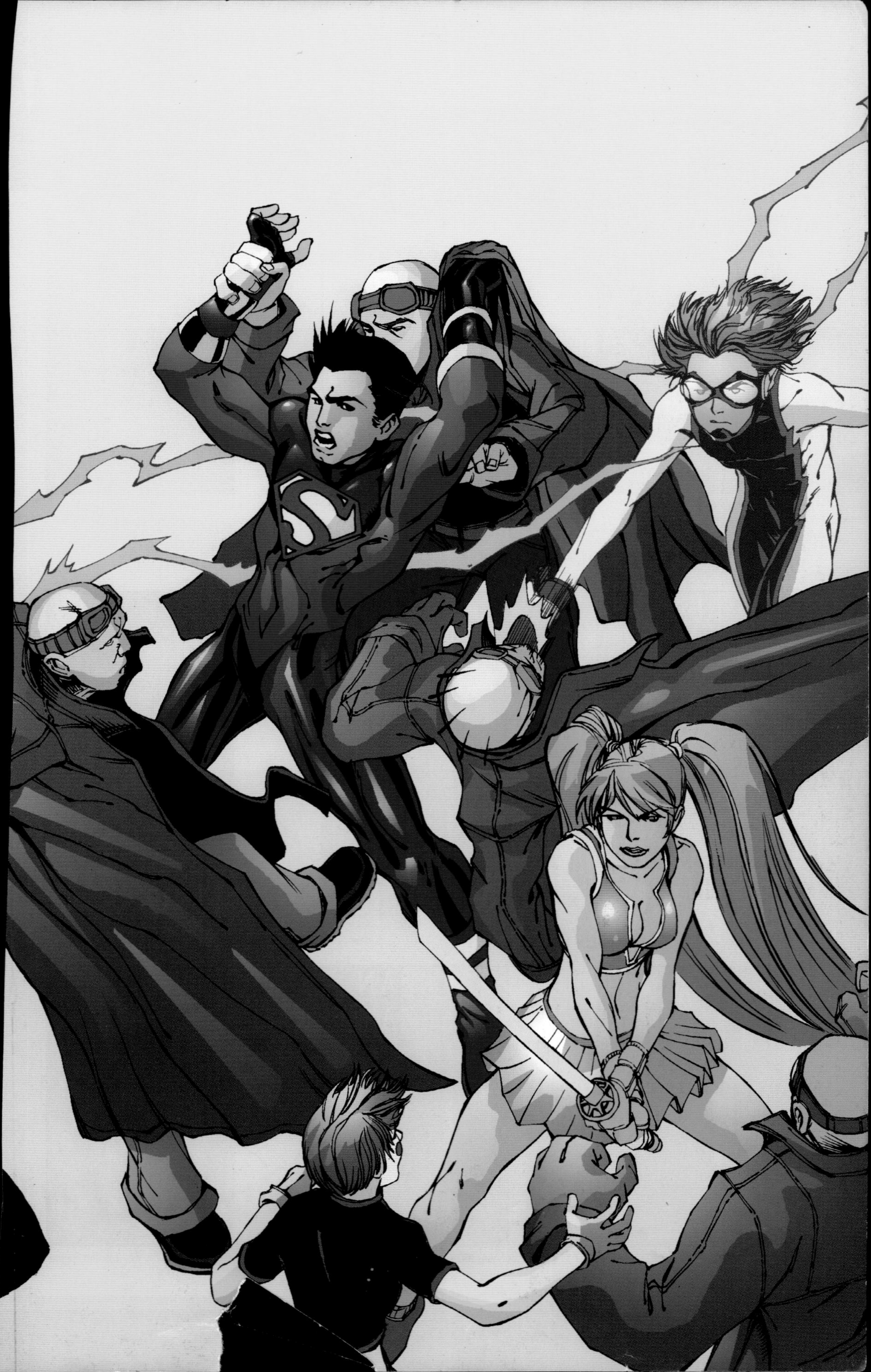

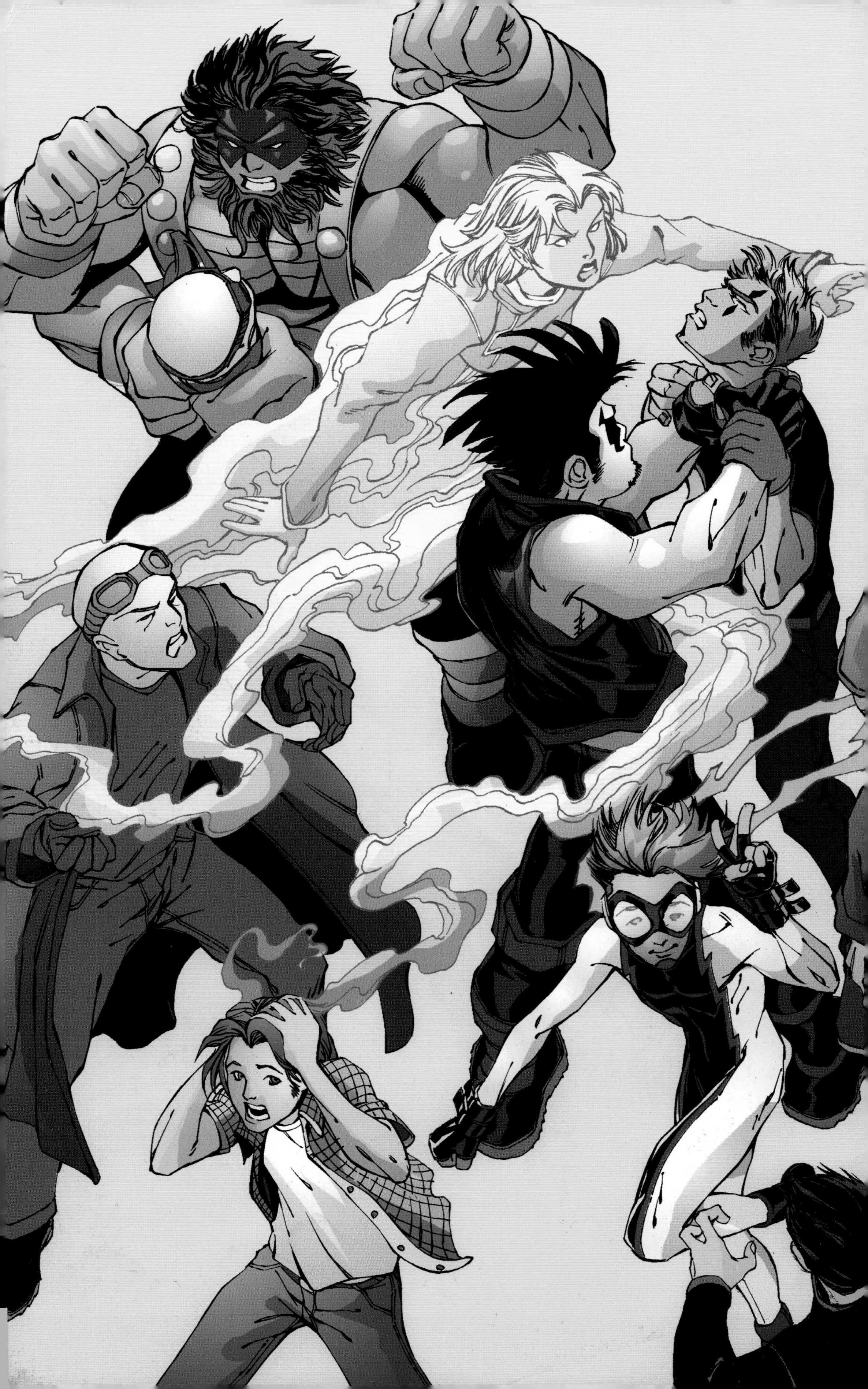

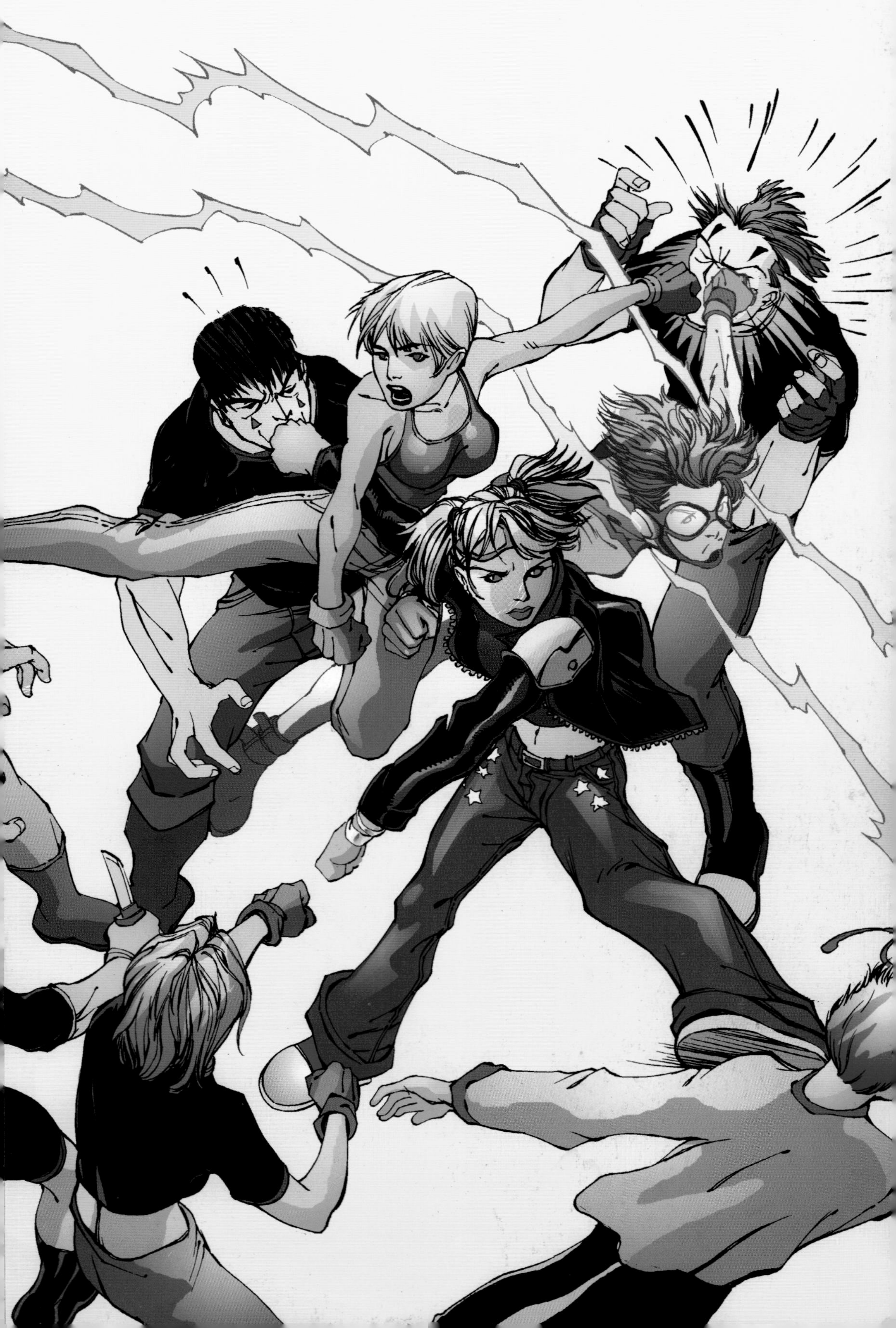

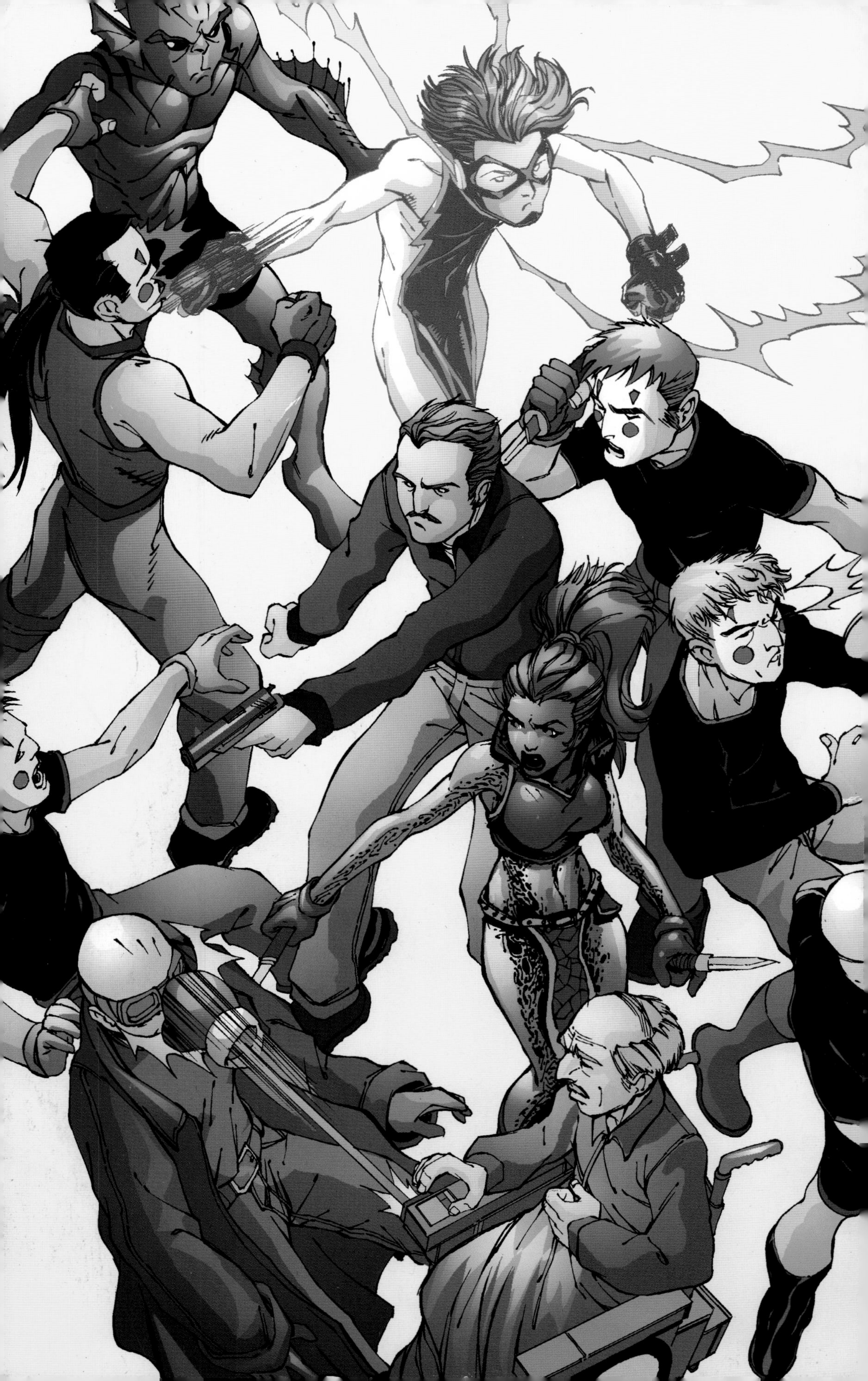

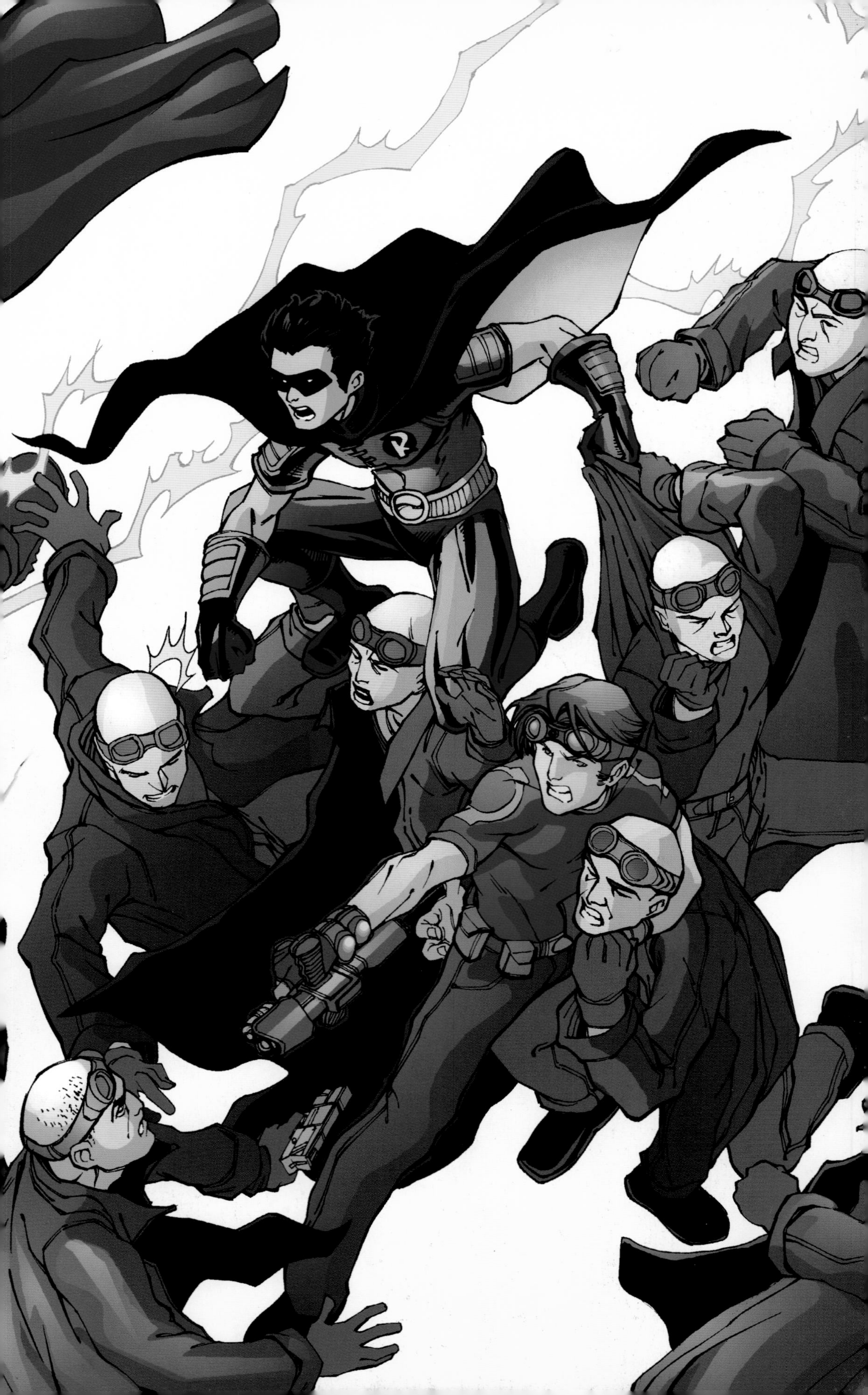